Mary Hunt Kahlenberg and Anthony Berlant

The Navajo Blanket

Praeger Publishers, Inc.
in association with the
Los Angeles County Museum of Art

Participating Museums

Los Angeles County Museum of Art
June 27–August 27, 1972

Fall 1972–Spring 1976

Navajo Tribal Museum, Window Rock, Arizona

The Brooklyn Museum

Institute for the Arts, Rice University

William Rockhill Nelson Gallery of Art
Atkins Museum of Fine Arts, Kansas City

Institute of Contemporary Arts, London

Kunstverein Hamburg

The Detroit Institute of Arts

Des Moines Art Center

The Art Institute of Chicago

Portland Art Museum, Portland, Oregon

Brooks Memorial Art Gallery, Memphis

Royal Ontario Museum, Toronto

Stedelijk Museum, Amsterdam

List Incomplete

Group portrait taken about 1877, standing left to right: Captain Frank Bennett, unknown Navajo, Cayetanito, sitting: Juanita, Manuelito; courtesy of Museum of New Mexico

Cover:
Serape Style Blanket, 1840–1860
Southwest Museum, Los Angeles
Catalog number 12, page 34

Title Page:
Navajo wrestler, about 1879; courtesy of Smithsonian Institution, National Anthropological Archives, Bureau of American Ethnology Collection

Library of Congress
Catalog Card Number 79–189549

ISBN 0 87587 050 3

Published by
Praeger Publishers, Inc.
in association with the
Los Angeles County Museum of Art

Second printing, 1973

Table of Contents

Lenders to the exhibition

The American Museum of Natural History, New York

Arizona State Museum, The University of Arizona, Tucson

Anthony Berlant, Santa Monica, California

William H. Claflin, Boston

The Denver Art Museum, Native Arts Collection

Field Museum of Natural History, Chicago

Byron Harvey, Phoenix

The Heard Museum, Phoenix

Jasper Johns, New York

Donald Judd, New York

Lowe Art Museum, Alfred I. Barton Collection, Coral Gables, Florida

The Maxwell Collection, Maxwell Museum of Anthropology University of New Mexico, Albuquerque

Museum of Navajo Ceremonial Art, Inc., Santa Fe

Natural History Museum of Los Angeles County

Navajo Tribal Museum, Window Rock, Arizona

Kenneth Noland, New York

Georgia O'Keeffe, Abiquiu, New Mexico

Millicent A. Rogers Memorial Museum, Inc., Taos, New Mexico

School of American Research Collection in the Museum of New Mexico, Santa Fe

Southwest Museum, Los Angeles

Frank Stella, New York

Taylor Museum of the Colorado Springs Fine Arts Center

The University Museum, University of Pennsylvania, Philadelphia

Thomas Woodard, Gallup, New Mexico

Acknowledgments

In 1931 John Sloan and Oliver LaFarge wrote in the introduction to the catalog of "the first exhibition of American Indian Art selected entirely with consideration of aesthetic value," an exhibition circulated by the College Art Association: "We white Americans have been painfully slow to realize the Indian's value to us and to the world as an independent artist." So slow, in fact, that forty years later this exhibition of Navajo blankets is still a pioneering effort in securing art museum recognition for the Indian's artistic achievements.

At the same time that the arts of Africa, the South Pacific, and Pre-Columbian Middle and South America have been widely exhibited in art museums across the country, and even added to their permanent collections, the art of the Indians of the United States and Canada has remained almost the exclusive province of the natural history and specialized ethnic museums. Following the 1931 exhibition, there have been only two comprehensive shows in art museums: *Indian Art of the United States* at the Museum of Modern Art in 1941 and *Two Hundred Years of North American Art,* restricted to painting and sculpture, at the Whitney Museum in 1971. There have also been a small number of exhibitions of Northwest Coast Art. During these same decades American Indian art has been part of the permanent collections of only four of the larger general art museums.

Consequently, when Tony Berlant, Los Angeles artist and noted collector of Navajo blankets, suggested the present exhibition, his proposal was accepted with great enthusiasm by Mary Hunt Kahlenberg, Curator of Textiles and Costumes at the Los Angeles County Museum of Art. To his artist and collector eye, she added her own connoisseurship and her knowledge of the history and technology of textiles. Together they made a careful survey of all accessible public and private collections in the country and from them selected this exhibition. Their aim was to prepare a comprehensive historical survey of nineteenth century Navajo weaving through objects of the highest technical and aesthetic merit.

In the name of the authors and of the participating institutions, I would like to thank the museums, universities, and private collectors who have generously provided the content of the exhibition as well as those who made their collections accessible for study. In particular, we wish to acknowledge our debt to those who have shared their knowledge of the Navajo and his art: Mabel O'Dell, Carl Dentzel, E. Boyd Hall, Martin Link, Martha Tilley, and Joseph Ben Wheat. We also wish to express our gratitude to Michael Barlow and Joanne Jaffe for editorial assistance, to Jeanne Doyle for having brought the catalog to completion, and to the staff of the Textiles and Costumes Department of the Los Angeles County Museum of Art: Catherine Dimmick, Nola Ewing, Florence Karant, and Mimi Zucker, and to the many others who helped enable us to present for the first time in depth one of the high points of American Indian art in an art museum.

KENNETH DONAHUE, *Director.*

Foreword

One may well wonder what sort of people are the Navajos (the *Dînéh)* who have woven these superlative blankets. What is their origin, where do they live, how do they work? Somewhat obscured in mystery, these Athapascan-speaking Indians are the latest Indian migration to reach the southwestern part of the United States, arriving some time about the middle of the sixteenth century and settling for a while in the region known as Old Navajo Land, near the junction of the Pine and San Juan rivers in the central part of southern Colorado and northern New Mexico. Traces of their early habitat have been found here. Archaeologists have also found the remains of dwellings built by the Pueblo people who had been living here many years before the arrival of the Navajos. Here, too, the Navajos encountered new domesticated animals brought to the Southwest by the Spanish Conquistadores a century earlier—horses which could be ridden and sheep whose wool could be used for weaving. Garments made of wool were worn by the Pueblos, and soon the Navajos were also wearing them. Most authorities on weaving believe that the Navajos learned their weaving skill from these new neighbors.

It was not long before the Navajos wanted horses and sheep of their own, trading for them when they had something to trade, stealing when this seemed the only way to such acquisition. Horses made the Navajos mobile. As the years went by and the Navajos became stronger and more numerous, the occasional raids upon the Pueblo people and even the Spanish villages along the Rio Grande became more frequent. The Navajos thus increased their flocks of sheep and their herds of horses. Gradually they moved toward the west, building their simple homes, or hogans, moving on to better pastures for their stock, exploring this rugged and beautiful land. By the end of the eighteenth century, word of these people had reached far and wide, even to Spain, and in many of the reports their weaving skill was spoken of with admiration.

Because they needed good pasturage for their sheep, the Navajos became a semi-nomadic people, living in groups or clans in what is now northwestern New Mexico and northeastern Arizona. Existing quite independently, they had no central government, but each group was led by a head man. When one group made some sort of treaty with the Spanish government, it in no way affected another group under another leader. This was the situation when the government of the United States acquired the Southwest following the war with Mexico in 1846. Raids continued, and finally the famous scout Kit Carson was sent out to quell the Navajos. Colonel Carson did not bring outright war to these Indians but subdued them by killing their stock and burning their crops and finally by rounding up a large portion of the tribe in Canyon de Chelly, that maze of small canyons in Arizona. So, in 1864 the conquered Navajos were marched to Fort Sumner, on the Pecos River in New Mexico, some three hundred miles from their homeland. Here, along with a group of Apaches, the Navajos were held prisoner for four long and disastrous years. An epidemic of small pox wiped out hundreds, and drought and insect infestations destroyed their crops. Finally they were allowed to return to their own country, where they signed a treaty with the government of the United States. They had been promised aid to start a new life; they were to receive seed, a few simple tools, and three sheep per family, but nothing was delivered until late in 1869. This was too late to plant crops, and for nearly two years they existed on what they could find, rebuilding their hogans and literally living off the land. But exist they did, and they grew into the strong and independent individuals we know today.

Perhaps it is the long years of outdoor life, the deprivation, and the hardships they endured that have instilled such vitality and character in their art. Perhaps from the necessities of their lives come the strengths and ideas for their bold and beautiful designs which are woven with such consummate skill. Living even more closely to nature than their urban Pueblo neighbors, they know intimately all phases of climate, of drought, of storm, and ensuing hardships and have put this knowledge to the best use they know how.

Like their physiques, their looms are upright. The looms are easy to assemble and reassemble when moving is necessary. Unlike most weavers, they carry the designs of these magnificent textiles in their minds with never a mark or a drawing. Seldom are patterns duplicated. Always there are new shapes, new patterns, new combinations of color, new uses of old figures, a variety that can be matched only by the earth and sky in their ever-changing moods of light.

Until recent years, simplicity has marked Navajo life. Because they have long been shepherds, pasture is of prime importance to them. Therefore, their homes are scattered far and wide across the country. Small clusters of hogans, few in number, are the homes of families, and they are separated by land upon which their sheep may graze. Designed by the mythological personage, the Changing Woman, hogans are usually round or hexagonal in shape with a conical roof; they are built of the material nearest at hand—log, or stone, or combinations of these. Always the door faces East, to the rising sun and the new day. To the right as one enters are the cooking utensils, and in the center of the roof is a smoke hole with an open fire beneath, although in present times one finds many stoves and stove pipes. The round, or nearly round, shape of the building holds heat with the least amount of fuel. The fuel, usually wood, is often hauled from a distance. Wind and storm do less damage to rounded shapes than to square corners and joints. At the rear of the hogan rolls of bedding, usually sheepskins, are stacked during the day. Containers, suitcases or boxes for clothes, small possessions, and ceremonial objects are stacked nearby. There will doubtless be a pile or sack of wool waiting to be carded and spun. Hanging from the roofbeams near the walls will be skeins of dyed wool ready for weaving. Somewhere will be kept a container of plant and mineral substances gathered to make dyes for the wool. In winter the woman's loom will be set up within the hogan, while in warm weather the loom will be outdoors under a brush shelter. Here the weaver can see distant horizons, or activities near at hand, or the slow movement of grazing sheep herded by a child, while her busy hands work the weft through the warp and the design assumes its final harmony. Laura Gilpin

Spider Woman instructed the Navajo women how to weave on a loom which Spider Man told them how to make. The crosspoles were made of sky and earth cords, the warp sticks of sun rays, the healds of rock crystal and sheet lightning. The batten was a sun halo, white shell made the comb. There were four spindles: one a stick of zigzag lightning with a whorl of cannel coal; one a stick of flash lightning with a whorl of turquoise; a third had a stick of sheet lightning with a whorl of abalone; a rain streamer formed the stick of the fourth, and its whorl was white shell.

NAVAJO LEGEND

Navajo weaver; courtesy of Southwest Museum

History

The visual impact of Navajo blankets conveys the strength of Navajo culture and their tradition as a people. The story of the *Dinéh* ("The People of the Earth," the term the Navajos use to refer to themselves) is only partially documented and certainly cannot be adequately described in a few pages. What we have tried to provide, therefore, is a general sketch—one we hope will help to place Navajo blankets in the larger context of Navajo history. A fuller discussion of the events touched on here can be found in the standard references: Ruth M. Underhill's book *The Navajos* is particularly recommended as a readable and intelligent survey, and John Upton Terrell's *The Navajos: Past and Present of a Great People* provides valuable historical detail.

The history of the Navajo tribe, as we know it, extends over only the last six or seven hundred years. Along with their relatives, the Apaches, they were late arrivals to the Southwest. Authorities believe their ancestors may have migrated from northwestern Canada about 1000 A.D.

Little is recorded about the Navajos before the white man entered their lands; earlier times are remembered only in the myths and legends of the tribe itself.

Those historical records which date from as early as the seventeenth century reveal the Navajos' response to a number of great changes, events that destroyed other tribes and nations. The Navajos did more than survive; there is a pattern of change peculiar to them—an ability to absorb the lessons and skills of alien cultures, to adapt and improve upon them, and yet retain their own individuality.

The Navajos are now the largest single Indian tribe in the United States. The tribe has grown greatly in size since it was placed in reservations. As craftsmen and farmers, they have adapted more successfully to reservation life than members of most other tribes. Their way of life contrasts sharply with that of the Navajos during the first half of the nineteenth century. A powerful, autonomous tribe known as the "Lords of the Soil," whose raiding warriors profited from attacks on other Indians, as well as on the Spanish, they were independent of the white man's control but not of the benefits of cultural contact. Spanish goods, traded with the Pueblos at Santa Fe, indirectly supplied the Navajos with wool materials that came to play a key role in the development of their weaving. The reputation of their blankets, woven by the women of the tribe, matched that of the Navajo men for their skill as warriors. The blankets were considered marks of honor by chiefs of other tribes, and their quality was appreciated by the Spanish as well.

In the spring of 1846, the rule in Santa Fe changed hands. As a result of the Mexican War the United States took control of the southwest territories almost without military incident. The Spanish either fled or surrendered when General Kearny and his troop of Missouri volunteers arrived. Peace was established and citizens were given the same rights they had held under the Spanish, including protection against Indian raids and restoration of stolen property. A council was held where the Indians were told of the new administration and laws. A permanent peace treaty was signed—signed, that is, by tribes other than the Navajos, who did not attend the council and responded to the new laws with a raid on the Rio Grande Pueblos. For the next fifteen years, the situation remained essentially the same. Expeditions were sent to the Navajos, gifts made to encourage them to adopt the new ways, "lasting" peace treaties agreed to, but the Navajo raids continued.

Prejudice and romantic popular histories have obscured the fact that few Navajo men were actually raiders. But, since the tribe did not have a social structure that gave control to a single "chief," treaties were useless in stopping the bands from the north who were responsible for most of the attacks. When retaliation against the Navajo raids came, it often fell most heavily on the members of the tribes who were most accessible—those who had not been raiders at all.

In 1861 even these ineffectual efforts to tame the Navajos were discontinued, and the American troops were sent off to a larger struggle, leaving only a skeleton guard in the Navajo country. In September, 1862, Brigadier General James H. Carleton was appointed Commander of the New Mexico Territory. He believed the only way to deal with the Navajos was to make them feel "that they have been doing wrong," and to convince them of this by forcing them to change their way of life completely. In a letter to the Adjutant General in Washington he stated his intent:

> The purpose now is never to relax the application of force with a people who can no more be trusted than you can trust the wolves that run through their mountains; to gather them together, little by little, on to a reservation away from their haunts, and hills, and the hiding places of their country; and then to be kind to them; there teach their children how to read and write; teach them the arts of peace; teach them the truths of Christianity.
>
> Soon they will acquire new habits, new ideas, new modes of life; the old Indians will die off, and carry with them all latent longings for murdering and robbing; the young ones will take their place without these longings; and thus, little by little, they will become a happy and contented people, and Navajo wars will be remembered only as something that belongs entirely to the past.[1]

Carleton proposed destroying the culture and rebuilding it by means of idealism and paternalism. The famous "Indian fighter," Colonel Kit Carson, Commander of the first New Mexico volunteers, first took his men on a campaign against the Mescalero Apaches. After a few months of battle, the Apaches surrendered. Four hundred of the tribe were transported to the barren southeast corner of New Mexico and held there at Fort Sumner.

In June, 1863, Kit Carson and his volunteers began the campaign against the Navajos. He lacked sufficient horses and supplies, and his troops never numbered more than eight hundred men. Carleton's orders were to subdue the Navajos, a tribe then numbering more than ten thousand members. The campaign lasted only six months. Carson's victory was clear-cut.

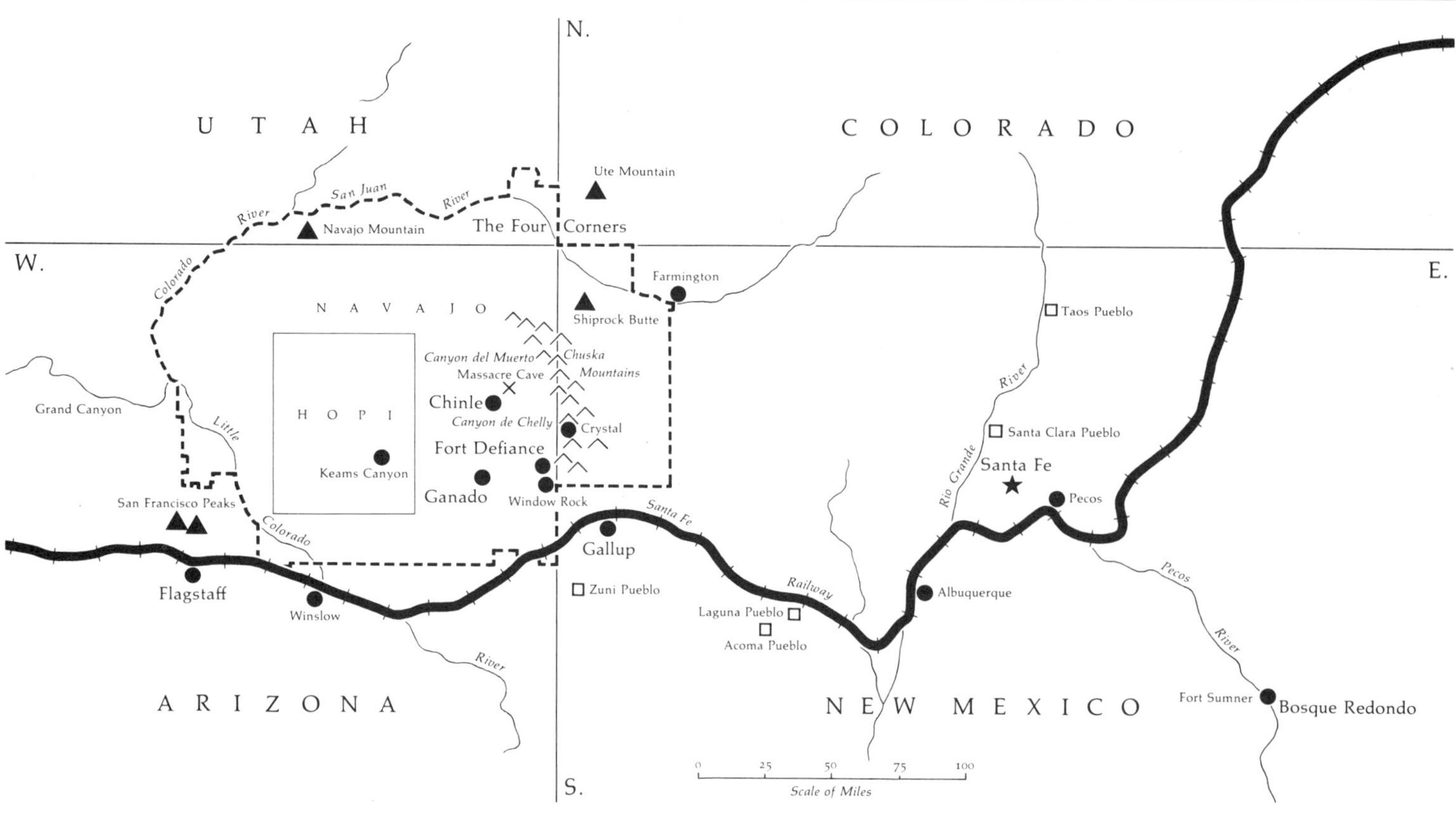

8

What made it possible was aid from the other Indian tribes who saw this as an opportunity to settle old scores in full measure and to profit from their revenge by taking sheep, horses, and slaves. Kit Carson won without open battle: as the Ute and Pueblos raided, the soldiers burned their crops and homes, and the Navajos were forced into hiding and surrender. Few Navajos were killed in battle, but the total destruction of their herds and crops, combined with a brutal winter, brought the scattered tribe to their first defeat. They faced hopeless starvation. When promised rations at the American Fort Defiance, most of them surrendered. Scattered and isolated bands continued to resist, but under continued hardship many of them finally capitulated.

Then came what the Navajos still refer to as the "long walk," three hundred miles to their new home at Fort Sumner. The journey progressed at a rate of only fifteen miles each day. Eight and a half thousand Navajos survived the walk only to encamp on an arid forty square miles of featureless landscape distinguished by just a circular grove of cottonwood trees. Bosque Redondo, Spanish for "round grove," is the name given in Navajo history to the place as well as to the period of exile. Irrigation ditches were dug and crops were planted; sheep were few. The military faced social and psychological problems with their tenants, and these problems were to lead directly to economic and cultural ones. Appropriations for aid from Washington were slow, difficult, and insufficient to support the Navajos.

Carleton had underestimated the number of Navajos who would surrender. And at Bosque Redondo the agricultural resources and supplies were totally inadequate to support its inhabitants. He pleaded eloquently for additional supplies with a War Department preoccupied with the pressures of the Civil War. He also tried to curtail the growing business among New Mexicans of trade in Navajo slaves. Carleton's pleas and orders, however, were more noteworthy for their eloquence than for their effectiveness. At the Bosque, hundreds of Navajos died of hunger and disease. Many lived in holes dug in the ground, covered by brush and debris. Clothes were scarce. This was the "training ground" where the Navajos were to learn the arts of peace.

Although agriculture was constantly encouraged, tools sufficient to the purpose were not genrally available. The hard soil could not be broken by ordinary plows, and the irrigation ditches were virtually dug by hand.

Carleton also had a master plan for the housing of the Navajos, and he ordered the building of a pueblo-like series of adobe houses. The Navajo fear of contamination by the dead was at first discounted in this plan, but when the Indians held firm to their belief a compromise was attempted. The traditional hogans would be arranged in long rows like city blocks. When a death occurred, a family could move to the end of the row and there build a new hogan. The dubious results of this unique city plan were never fully experienced because too many other areas of life at Bosque Redondo were disintegrating. Public criticism of Carleton—and more important, intra-War Department resentment over his unapproved initiative—grew more powerful. Scandals involving the sale of government property and supplies were revealed.

After four desperate years, Lieutenant General W. T. Sherman was sent to review the situation. In a letter to his brother, he described Bosque Redondo:

> We found 7200 Indians there, seemingly abject and disheartened. They have been there four years. The first year, they were maintained by the army at a cost of about $700, 000, and made a small crop. The second year the cost was about $500,000, and the crop was small. Last year the crop was an utter failure, though all the officers say they labored hard and faithfully. This year they would not work because they said it was useless. . . .
>
> Now this was the state of facts, and we could see no time in the future when this could be amended. The scarcity of wood, the foul character of the water, which is salty and full of alkali, their utter despair, made it certain we would have to move them or they would scatter and be a perfect nuisance. So of course we concluded to move them. After debating all the country at our option, we have chosen a small part of their own country, which is as far out of the way of the whites and our future probable wants as possible, and have agreed to move them there forthwith.[2]

The Navajos were permitted to return to their lands after they had signed a treaty promising never again to fight with whites, Mexicans, or Indians—a promise the tribe has kept. But the confidence and decisiveness of the free-roaming life was gone. On their restricted territory thc Navajos were more susceptible to the full impact of white culture, and their weaving could not help but be affected. At Bosque Redondo, stylistic and technical changes in the making of their blankets began. The pride with which a blanket was woven and worn lessened. Nevertheless, the women continued their traditional methods throughout the decades following 1860. Although the period of full autonomy and assurance was over, the changes that came in response to direct contact with Americans were in their own way as vital and as exciting as earlier periods.

The experience of the Navajos at Bosque Redondo has strong parallels with another key event in their development—the Pueblo Revolt of 1680. Much as other Indian tribes profited from the American subjugation of the rebel Navajos, the Navajos had gained immensely from the punishment the Spanish had inflicted on the Pueblo tribe. In fact, much of what we consider central to Navajo culture—including the art of weaving—had been learned from the Pueblos during this period.

The Navajos and the Apaches have common origins in a wandering branch of the Athapascan tribe of northwest Canada. Markedly different in language from the tribes who had settled earlier in the Southwest, this ancestor brought from the north a powerful new tool—a sinew-backed bow of greater accuracy and strength than the simple weapons used by other tribes of the Southwest.

It has been theorized that the attacks of the wandering, warlike Navajos were a major reason for the close, city-like cliff-dwellings the Pueblos adopted. The Navajos were at this time a tribe too mobile to become involved in agriculture and were without elaborate crafts. They dressed in clothing of hides and roamed much of the Southwest Territory—the land "between the four mountains"—in search of game. Eventually, they began to exhaust the supply of animals and turned more and more to another means of support: raids on other tribes. Raids produced not only food but slaves as well. This was one of the ways in which the Pueblos began to be absorbed into the Navajo culture. The other main means of assimilation was intermarriage, arranged by dowry. Most anthropologists agree that this intermingling of the tribes was the beginning of much of what is considered Navajo culture—their ceremonies, crafts, and agricultural methods.

Don Juan de Oñate, appointed Governor and Captain General of New Mexico by the King of Spain, in 1598 began an expedition into the Southwest. He had been authorized by the King "to distribute land among the colonists, to accept the submission of the Indians, and to see that—for the good of their souls—they rendered homage to both the King of Spain and the Christian God."[3]

Oñate came with his horses, his men in armor, sixty-two oxcarts, and 7,000 domestic animals, including 1,000 head of cattle, 3,000 sheep, 1,000 goats, 150 colts, and 150 mares.[4] This display had its intended effect on the Pueblos; by 1610, they had lost their freedom.

Although the Spanish claimed the territory occupied by the Navajos as well, the Navajos did not become a subject people. In fact, they profited from the arrival of the invader and his marvelous new animals. Hidden in their remote canyons, the Navajos were known to the Spanish, but there was no great concern over their salvation or subjugation. It was safer to leave the Navajos alone.

The Pueblos, by contrast, lived under an increasingly oppressive Spanish rule. Endangered as well by Navajo raids on their newly acquired animals, the Pueblos made a number of abortive attempts to free themselves. Each failed, and after each attempt, their ardor for freedom grew. Finally, in August, 1860, the Pueblos united with the Apaches and drove the Spanish back down the Rio Grande. The fast retreat left numerous sheep and horses abandoned. The Navajos, on the fringes of the conflict, gained what they could.

Although they benefited from the Pueblo Revolt, it was not until the Spanish returned in 1692 that the Navajos became the most powerful and richest of the Southwest Indians. When the Spanish returned in full force to regain their territory and their rule, the Pueblos hopelessly trapped, either surrendered or were destroyed. Many of them were forced into slavery. Still others fled, and a great number of these went to join the Navajos. The people of entire Pueblo villages spent several years among the Navajos before it was safe to return. Intermarriage became a common occurrence, and as a result the Navajos incorporated many elements of Pueblo life into their own developing culture. The Pueblo influence was of lasting significance.

Pueblo ceremony was community-oriented, with prayers meant to bring blessings upon a whole village. While Pueblo prayers dealt with the individual as a part of his community, the Navajos, more isolated and independent, prayed for personal strength and power.

Among the Pueblos men were the weavers, but in the Navajo tribe this craft passed into the hands of women. Navajo men, accustomed to a life of hunting and battle, did not adopt the complicated art of weaving. Among the Navajo women weaving rapidly grew as a key and distinctive skill. Although the Navajos possessed some sheep before the Pueblo Revolt, the large number gathered by the tribe at that time rooted weaving in their culture.

Throughout the eighteenth century, the Navajos spread away from their remote canyons into the plateau country, part of which is still their reservation. They surrounded the Hopi and the Zuni and made raids on the Spanish settlements. Their ferocious reputation grew along with their wealth. With a great number of sheep and a growing prosperity, Navajo women had time to devote to refinement of their weaving skill. At first they duplicated Pueblo styles, but it appears that they soon developed a weaving style of their own. In 1795 Governor Fernando de Chacon remarked in a letter: "They have increased their horse herds considerably, they sow much and on good fields; they work their wool with more delicacy and taste than the Spanish."[5] In his *Exposición de Nuevo México* (1812), Pedro Pino, delegate to the Spanish Parliament from New Mexico, wrote of the Navajos: "Their woolen fabrics are the most valuable in our province, and Sonora . . . and Chihuahua as well."[6]

The earliest surviving Navajo blankets date from the late-eighteenth and early-nineteenth centuries. Most of these are fragments found in caves, and the most significant of them were found in a place in the Cañon del Muerto, remembered in Navajo history as Massacre Cave. Because it can only be reached by climbing to the top of a rocky cliff and then sliding down into the mouth of the cave, it was a perfect hiding place for the Navajos during the occasional retaliatory attacks mounted by the Spanish. In 1805 during a series of these attacks when Navajo families were hiding from nearby Spanish troops, the story has it that a woman, thinking the cave absolutely safe, let out a cry of revenge. The location was revealed, and the Spanish climbed to a point on the rocks close to the cave firing bullets that richocheted off the cliff into the hiding place. All the Indians in the cave were either killed or captured. Afraid of spiritual contamination by the dead, the Navajo tribe never again entered this refuge.

Even though treasure hunters occasionally ventured into the cave, when it was finally entered by anthropologists, it yielded valuable evidence of Navajo life at the time of the massacre. Woven fragments were found that provide us with our clearest idea of what their weaving was like. A section of a stripe-pattern wearing blanket *(plate 3)* was the largest fragment found.[7] It is coarsely woven wool entirely in natural colors. Smaller fragments reveal finer weaving. One such example, in the collection of William Claflin, Jr., has a white ground with a beaded black stripe and three composite stripes (black center outlined in reddish brown, bordered by four-ply unraveled red yarn, very fine weave).[8] These few specimens from Massacre Cave indicate the inventiveness, range, and skill of Navajo women in weaving and establish their reputation for design beyond that of the Pueblos who had taught them.

Navajo Captive at Bosque Redondo; courtesy of Arizona Historical Society Library

Notes on Technique and Materials

Natural Wool Colors. There are two natural wool colors, white and brown. The white is creamy, and the brown varies in range from dark to almost black. By carding the two colors together a great variation within the brown-blacks is possible. Often this combination produces grey tones.

Bayeta. The Spanish name for English baize, bayeta was a flannel fabric woven in many colors. Shipped via Spain to the New World, it was used there as a trade item. It was the Pueblos who then traded bayeta to the Navajos. The favorite color for export was red, and the particular red (scarlet and blue-red) used in Navajo blankets was achieved by dyeing the fabric with cochineal. Before using bayeta in their blankets the Navajos had to cut it into strips, unravel it, and hand-twist the strands together. As tedious as this sounds, it was probably easier and quicker than spinning their own wool to the same level of fineness. The term bayeta is used to refer to all natural dyed unraveled yarns as well as to English baize.

American Flannel. After the Americans had arrived in the Southwest, they realized the desirability of importing a red cloth that could be unraveled. This cloth, called American flannel, replaced bayeta. The term generally refers to an aniline-dyed fabric of lesser quality which can be distinguished from bayeta by its aniline orange-red color. Frequently these red yarns had to be carded and respun.

Saxony. Probably the first commercial yarns available to the Navajos, Saxony yarns were imported from Germany and were brought to the Southwest as early as 1850. Some were retraded to the Navajos. Amsden suggests that during their captivity at Bosque Redondo the Navajos, deprived of their flocks, obtained commercial yarns from the soldiers.[9] Saxony is a fine yarn found primarily in blankets from 1860 to 1880. It is characterized by its soft color, silky texture, and most importantly by the fact that it is usually three-ply. Saxony reds were often combined with unraveled bayeta in blankets. Although the most common Saxony colors are red, blue, green, and white, in a few blankets there is a much wider range of Saxony colors.

Germantown. An American four-ply, machine-spun yarn, Germantown was named for its original place of manufacture in Pennsylvania. The Navajos began to use this yarn in the late 1870s and employed it extensively for the next thirty years. Germantown yarns were available in a wide range of colors that were previously inaccessible. To use many of them together was frequently an irresistible temptation. Because Germantown was a finely-spun plied yarn, blankets woven from it are very even in texture and stiffer than those of soft handspun wool. Other three-ply aniline-dyed yarns can occasionally be seen in blankets before the late 1870s.

Native Natural Dyes. Although a range of native dyes is found in rugs woven by the Navajos today, these dyes, despite what is commonly believed, were rarely used before the present "revival" period. Very few early blankets show evidence of native dyes even though such dyes were used in the Southwest in baskets and cotton textiles beginning in the basket-maker period. Dyes for coloring vegetable matter, however, do not always produce the same results on animal fibers.

Yellow. Yellow is another color recognizable in pre-aniline blankets. Three sources of native yellow are commonly given: a bright yellow or yellow-green was obtained from the flowers of the rabbit weed or brush *(Bigelovia graveolens);* an orange-yellow from the roots of canyorgre *(Rumex hymenosepalus);* and a bright yellow from the blossoms and twigs of chamizo *(Attriplex canescerns).* Green was made by combining rabbit weed and indigo.

Red. There is some disagreement about the source of red. Indeed there are native sources of red in the Southwest, but none of these produces a color sufficiently strong for dyeing wool. One in particular, a combination of the bark of the *Alnus incana* variety of virescens, the bark of the root *Cercocarpus parvifolius,* and a mordant of fine juniper ashes produces a dull red when used to dye wool and a brighter red as a dye for skins.

Indigo. Blue corn and blue clay may have been native blue dyes, although neither was used after the Spanish introduced Mexican indigo. Indigo was brought by mule train to the Spanish villages along the upper Rio Grande and from this point probably reached the Navajos by way of the Pueblos. A penetrating dye, indigo produces a strong and lasting color, and yet it has a soft tone that distinguishes it from the later purplish-blue aniline dyes. Fragments from Massacre Cave show the use of indigo, and it is very likely that the Navajos had been using it for some time. The strength of its color and the ease with which it was used—requiring no boiling—made it a popular dye even when aniline blues were available.

Cochineal. The red of cochineal has a bluish tint. The dye is a ground powder made from the cochineal beetle cultured in Mexico. It is rarely found on native handspun yarn, and although it could have been obtained in the same manner as indigo, its expense obviously made it prohibitive. It was, however, the basic dye used for bayeta. Its blue-red color distinguishes it immediately from the orange-red of the aniline dyes.

Aniline Dyes. In 1856 aniline dyes appeared on the market. These synthetically produced dyes made of coal tar products had an instantaneous effect on the use of color in fabrics throughout the world. By 1870 aniline dyes were in general use in America, and by 1880 they were common in Navajo blankets. However, there are a number of examples of blankets containing aniline-dyed yarns, both handspun and commercially spun, prior to this date.[10] Aniline dye was easy to use. It had only to be dropped, package and all, into a pot of boiling water and the yarn boiled until the desired color strength was attained. It was inexpensive and the range of colors endless compared to the existing Navajo palette. Many of these once-vibrant aniline colors have now faded to a mellowness resembling the quiet natural dyes. If the strands of wool are separated, however, one can see the unfaded color and imagine what the blanket would have originally looked like.

The Navajo Loom. The Navajo loom and the accessories used in weaving—the spindle, batten, shuttle, and comb—have changed very little since their development in prehistoric Pueblo days. The loom is slightly more than a rough frame built to the specifications of each new blanket. Two vertical posts, or even two slender trees growing at a convenient distance, are the main supports of the loom. Two other posts are then tied crosswise forming a rectangular frame. A second set of vertical beams is laid parallel on the ground. The warp, continuously strung between the two beams, defines the length and the width of the blanket. After the warp has been laid, this section is fastened inside the rectangular frame. String heddles (used to raise or lower the warp threads) provide a means of opening the first shed (a temporary space between the two planes of warp threads through which the yarn passes). The second shed is made by a single rod above the heddles. As each shed is opened so the yarn can be inserted, it is kept open by insertion of the batten. After the yarn is pulled through, the batten is pulled out and the yarn is beaten into place by a comb. When the weaving has progressed to a point where it can no longer be reached comfortably by the weaver, who is seated on the ground, the center frame is lowered and the section of the blanket which has been woven is sewn tightly to itself at the bottom. Traces of this sewing can be seen on many blankets. The blanket is not complete until it has been woven to the very top of the frame; the last few rows are laid in by hand.

One distinctive characteristic of Navajo weaving is the three twisted threads that form a braid along the four edges and catch every thread as it is laid in along the edge. In doing so these threads reinforce the blanket exactly where it is subjected to most strain; and by strengthening the selvage they also help to keep the blanket straight.

Preparation of the Wool. Until the turn of the century the Navajos sheared their sheep with a case knife. It was a crude and wasteful method. After shearing, the wool was not immediately washed, since water was so scarce. The only cleansing that took place consisted of shaking the wool to remove the sand and then placing it on bushes where the entangled burrs and sticks were pulled out by hand. In the 1880s when the government made sheep dipping compulsory, traders began to insist that the wool be washed.

After the wool had been cleaned, by whichever manner, it was carded. The individual tangled fibers were straightened as a brush was pulled through them. The brush was made of a wooden frame to which burrs were attached. After it had been carded, the wool was ready for spinning.

Spinning. Although shearing and carding have long since been revolutionized by the introduction of the white man's methods, spinning continues to be done today as it always has been. The most obvious reason for this is that the traditional Navajo method avoids the need for a cumbersome spinning wheel. Instead, the weaver uses a simple spindle consisting of a wooden shaft over which a wooden disk is slipped; the disk is attached approximately a quarter of the distance from the bottom. The woman sits on the ground as she spins. One end of the spindle rests on the ground to her right and leans against her thigh. Using the thigh for leverage, the right hand rolls the spindle. The pulling and twisting that result from the rolling create the yarn. Usually the yarn is spun more than once. Two spinnings generally produce a yarn sufficiently thick and tight to be used for the weft (the horizontal threads of a textile). A third spinning adds the strength and tightness needed for the warp (the vertical threads among which the weft threads are interwoven). Because the Navajos have no method of plying the yarn, they must achieve the amount of firmness and strength they require in a single strand. Usually just the amount of wool needed for weaving a blanket is prepared in advance.

Tapestry Weave. The technique used in making Navajo blankets is the tapestry weave. What distinguishes this weaving technique from others is that the weft threads, by virtue of their size and tension, completely conceal the warp threads. Only the color of the weft threads is visible, therefore, and color patterns are created by weaving the weft threads back and forth within a given area. The weft does not always extend the full width of the fabric but only as far as is needed to complete a particular area of color.

Navajo weaver taken at Bosque Redondo, about 1867; courtesy of Museum of New Mexico

Bound edge of tapestry weave

Wedge weave detail

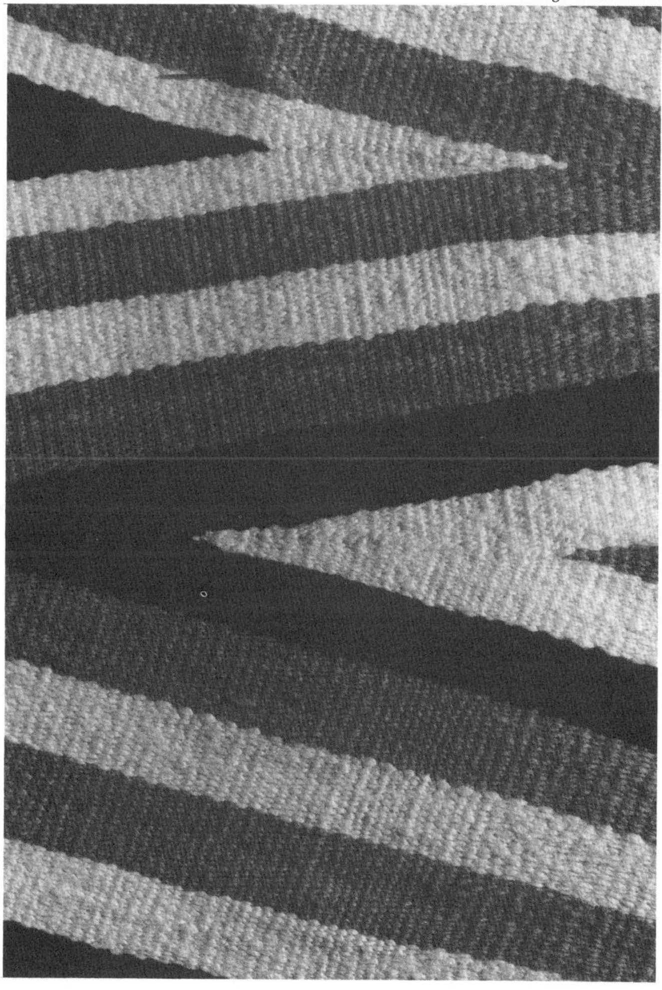

Wedge-Weave. Wedge-weave is a variation of the tapestry weave rather than a technique in its own right. It evolved as an easy method of creating a zigzag pattern. The diagonal build-up of the weft begins gradually and continues until the desired angle is achieved. The build-up produces tension on the warp threads pulling them toward the edge. At regular intervals the direction of the build-up is reversed resulting in a scalloped edge.

There are two other weaves which are not represented in the catalog: the twill weave and the double weave. Neither of these was common before the early twentieth century.

Lazy Lines. In weaving solid areas of color, the Navajos frequently use a device known as a lazy line. Rather than extend a continuous weft yarn the full length of the blanket, the weaver works in sections she can reach comfortably and completes one section before moving over to work on an adjacent area. In order to avoid breaks between sections, the inner edges of each area are slanted, and, because the join moves diagonally, there is rarely a break of more than a row. Lazy lines give a certain flexibility to the fabric and thus make it stronger.

Plain Stripe. The plain stripe blanket came directly from the Pueblo tradition and remained the most common style among the Navajos until the 1880s.

Banded Blanket. Banded blankets evolved from the plain stripe style when various design motifs were introduced into the area between the stripes.

Chief Pattern Blanket. The development of the chief pattern blanket can be divided into a first, second, and third phase. This division, however, provides only a genral framework, for there are many steps and variations within each phase. This style differs from that of all other Navajo blankets in that the warp runs the width rather than the length of the blanket.

Serape Style. Natural dyes were used in serape-style blankets, and the blanket patterns were based on the diamond motif of the Spanish. Traditionally these examples have been referred to as "classic" blankets. In our discussion of individual blankets the term serape style refers to blankets we believe were made before or during the Bosque Redondo period (1868). "Late serape style" is used to designate blankets of the period 1868–80. They mark the transition from serape to eye-dazzler style.

Eye-Dazzler. Eye-dazzler is a broad term for a style that developed with the introduction of aniline dyes. Blankets of both handspun and Germantown yarns are included in this category in which explosive color and design achieve an aggressiveness unknown in earlier periods.

Dating and Dyes. Specific information rarely remains to indicate the exact dates when a blanket was woven. From what is available, however, a chronology has been established, and from it dates can be approximated.

The greatest problems in dating concern the period before Bosque Redondo, an era in which examples are scarce and information non-existent. The stripe blankets, for example, remained unchanged from the Massacre Cave fragments to pieces collected sixty years later in the 1870s. Few examples of this type exist today, and those remaining give scant clues as to when in this sixty-year period they were woven. Circumstantial evidence indicates that bayeta serapes were not made before 1830, but no information dates them specifically between 1830 and early 1860.

As a rule aniline dyes did not come into widespread use until the arrival of the railroad in 1880. Blankets containing aniline-dyed yarns, both handspun and commercially spun, are found in the 1870s, and a few rare examples can be dated to the Bosque Redondo period.

Physical properties of the yarns—the dyes and spin—and the relationship of design, color, and proportion in an individual style allow us to date most pieces within a decade.

When a specific dye cannot be identified, the colors are listed as either native dyes (dyes indigenous to the Navajo area), or natural dyes (either non-aniline dyes imported for Navajo use or used on commercially-spun yarn).

Song of the Sky Loom

Oh our Mother The Earth, oh our Father The Sky,
Your children are we, and with tired backs
We bring you the gifts that you love.
Then weave for us a garment of brightness;
May the warp be the white light of morning,
May the weft be the red light of evening,
May the fringes be the falling rain,
May the border be the standing rainbow.
Thus weave for us a garment of brightness
That we may walk fittingly where birds sing,
That we may walk fittingly where the grass is green,
Oh our Mother The Earth, oh our Father The Sky![11] TEWA SONG

Two Navajos in 1890; courtesy of Arizona Historical Society Library

Stylistic Development

The fragments found in Massacre Cave provide evidence of the skill the Navajos possessed in weaving. These fragments are virtually the only known examples from the first 150 years of Navajo weaving following the Pueblo Revolt. Although the fragments are few in number, they give us enough information to establish the stylistic aspects of the Navajo blanket and its place in their culture.

The study and preservation of Navajo blankets is greatly indebted to Charles Avery Amsden, whose book *Navaho Weaving, Its Technic and Its History* is the classic work in the field. His pioneering scholarship is recommended for a more detailed discussion of technical and historical issues.

The shoulder blanket is only one of the types of woven items produced by the Navajos, but it holds pride of place in both design and in use. Other Navajo textiles include the woman's dress, saddle blankets, girths and throws, men's shirts, sashes, garters, leggings, and hair-cords. Among these, the woman's dress is of particular interest. Unlike the shoulder blanket, it was never produced for export, and it remained static in its conception, following closely the pattern of its Pueblo model. The woman's dress consists of two identically woven sections, sewn together on the sides, leaving an open area at the bottom for freedom of movement. It is also sewn across the shoulder area with openings at the sides for armholes. A belt or sash was usually worn to pull the dress tight at the waist. The Pueblo model, usually made in a twill weave, was of a single piece wrapped around the body under the left arm and fastened at the right shoulder. The Navajo two-piece construction probably derives from pre-weaving days when the skins of two deer were tied together as a dress.

Basic to the woven design of the woman's dress is a set of horizontal bands at the top and bottom of each panel. The earliest dresses were reported to have had borders of indigo blue with stripes of natural brown and black.[12] After the introduction of bayeta, small-scale red and blue patterns were worked into the borders. The weaving of a woman's dress is in the same technique as that of a shoulder blanket, and the two panels are always the same in design.

The shoulder blanket, also known as a wearing blanket, was made primarily to be worn by a member of the tribe; these blankets were also offered in trade with other tribes or with the white man. They are entirely secular objects and without ceremonial significance. Nor are these blankets symbolic in any direct sense. Efforts have been made to interpret blanket design symbolically, but these interpretations are imposed by the commentator. They are distinct from the way the Navajos saw the blanket in its original context. Each blanket is individual in design, and each represents both the woman who made it and the person who wears it in a vital way through the expression and control of its design. One of the best ways to understand the design of a Navajo wearing blanket is, very simply, to wear it. Draped like a cape and brought forward, pulled together across the arms, the essence of its design concept is revealed as half units meet to form whole units; elements break at just the right place, often following the lines of the arms. A central radiating point in the back is very typical, and this same form is often echoed in the front. The strong verticals reinforce the line of the spinal column.

From early photographs we know that blankets were worn draped in a great many ways depending on the activity and preference of the wearer. The need to keep warm while allowing movement resulted in endlessly improvised ways of wrapping the blankets. One might ask why this garment was draped when other garments were cut to the shape of the body. Doubtless it would have been difficult to cut and sew a fabric as heavy as a blanket. And had they done this, the effect would not have been as dramatic as that created by the design of the draped blanket. No matter how the blanket is worn, its design suits the body and de-emphasizes its physical reality, presenting an idealized being.

Blankets were also placed on the ground as a surface to sit on; however, they were never used as rugs. At night blankets, along with sheepskins, formed a bed, and the door to the hogan was often covered by a hanging blanket. Hung in this way, the blanket was experienced much like a painting, as it also was on the upright loom.

The blankets of the Navajos thus possessed a force beyond that customary for a single piece of apparel. They were made with care and concentration; in fact, there were Navajo ceremonies intended to restore the spirit of a woman who had spent too much time at the loom. Blankets represented both the tribe and the individual in a special way—not in a simple one-to-one symbolic relationship—but rather as a dynamic expression of the self. The word "blanket" is accurate, but its connotations in our society are too limited to suggest the versatility of what to the Navajos was almost a "second skin." The connection between the blanket and the role of the individual in society is one of the factors that makes their stylistic evolution in the nineteenth century so significant. This was the period of the first full interaction of Navajo culture with white society, and the spiritual and social reverberations of this contact can be sensed in the development of the blanket.

The stages of change in blanket styles can be categorized, but they are not firmly chronological. While there is an overall stylistic progression in the design of commonly worn stripe form from the simple to the complex, it is paradoxically true that, in the very early period, the rare bayeta serape form reached a complexity unmatched by even flamboyant late examples.

Plain Stripe. The majority of Navajos in the first three quarters of the nineteenth century wore blankets woven in the plain-stripe style. In early photographs these blankets are everywhere while other types are seen only occasionally. Despite the predominance of this style, otherwise outstanding museum collections often lack even a single example. Until recently they were thought to be blankets without design and with only historical interest.

The fineness of weave in these blankets varies from coarse and loose to very finely spun and woven examples. Broad bands of natural white yarn are defined by narrow bands of natural dark yarn, by thin stripes of indigo-dyed native yarn, and occasionally by unraveled material. Often the narrow bands were worked to create finely controlled variations in line so that their defining presence was felt more strongly. These blankets have a luminescent quality; the white areas appear as floating blocks of white color rather than as a negative ground. The subtle variation in modular scale and the energy contrasts resulting from the different colored yarns make a quietly controlled statement and yet build a forceful, frontal, unrelenting single image.

Frequently the narrow bands were made up of indigo and natural brown yarn so close in value that they produce a glowing, undulating sensation. The edges of the narrow bands define the shapes of the massive white blocks. The breadth and space these blankets contain and the uncanny blend of absolute calm with consistent, balanced energy mark them as a high point in the Navajo weaving tradition.

Early Serape Style—Bayeta Serape. Some time after 1830 a very ornate and elaborate style of blanket developed.[13] These blankets, known as bayeta serapes, were made in small numbers, and even in the earliest records we have of their existence they were considered rare and valuable. Probably they were made both as special items for trade with the Spanish and to be worn as a mark of honor and position within the tribe itself. The most spectacular examples are often made in the Mexican poncho style with a slit opening in the middle instead of being freely draped around the body. Another distinctive mark of these blankets is the abundance of unraveled Spanish trade material used to make them. The presence of bayeta, the Spanish name for the English fabric called baize, is especially notable. The Spanish brought large quantities of this common, multipurpose fabric to America, much of it to be used as a gift to the Indians to secure safe passage and to encourage peaceful trade.

Although available, bayeta rarely found its way directly from the Spanish into Navajo hands. More frequently it came by way of the Pueblos who had established commerce with the Spanish. There is a persistent myth, without factual basis, that the Navajos obtained bayeta from the uniforms of slain Spanish soldiers. While this is the kind of romantic "historical" anecdote that is often repeated, the story runs counter to the traditional Navajo avoidance of the dead and of their possessions for fear of spiritual contamination.

Speculation about the source of bayeta is of less interest than the inventive use the Navajos made of it. With the arrival of bayeta the Navajos' fame as weavers began. Bayeta was made in many colors, but the Navajos used the red almost exclusively. They unraveled sections of bayeta to obtain a yarn so finely spun that it served as an example to the Navajo spinner. The relative rarity and expense of this material generally meant that it had to be used with great restraint. This limitation brought with it aesthetic advantages. The contrast in visual quality between the native and the new foreign material was used in a way that heightened the effect of each. Used sparingly in a mosaic-like manner, bayeta added a new color and scale to Navajo blanket-making.

What prompted the Navajos to adopt the very different aesthetic shown in the bayeta serape? We know that the Navajos were exposed to complex pattern ideas in southwestern pottery and basketry, as well as in pictographic images; and their own sandpaintings were highly evolved in terms of design. In addition there were complicated prehistoric Pueblo textiles that closely resemble Navajo blankets, but with their fear of the dead, the Navajos probably never examined these.

Around 1830 the first terraced-diamond motif serapes came from Spain to the Spanish settlements of New Mexico, and the first examples of the Navajo bayeta serape are tentatively dated within the next twenty years. This evidence would seem to indicate that the Spanish example triggered the Navajos into a sudden extension of the earlier southwestern tradition and led them to break away from the vertical-horizontal grid.

The bayeta serape was an object produced to astound and impress. Fine, rare materials influenced the elaborateness of design and inspired weaving of the highest quality. Patterns in the bayeta serape literally burst across the blanket, and the energy of these blankets far surpassed that of their Spanish model. The design often appears as a variation of superimposed diamonds over stripes. Frequently the background is made of unraveled bayeta with horizontal stripes in blue and white; natural dyes of yellow and green were also used. Before Bosque Redondo the ornate diamond style was restricted to this rare hybrid, but as time passed the diamond came to rival the serene stripe as a basic motif.

The Chief Pattern Blanket. Less ornate in design than the bayeta serape, these blakets are equally impressive. They are woven with the warp running the width of the blanket as in the Pueblo cape style which was probably their antecedent. The term "chief blanket," found in the earliest commentaries, is something of a misnomer. There were no chiefs in the strict sense among the Navajos, and this type of blanket could have been worn by any member of the tribe. These blankets were often used in trade and might have acquired their name because they were owned by leaders of other tribes. Since they were usually very finely made and highly prized, chief pattern blankets customarily indicated a certain prestige among the Navajos.

The development of the chief pattern blanket can be divided into three main categories, although distinct variations can be seen within each of these. In the first phase the design consisted only of stripes. In the second phase nine rectangular blocks were inserted within the striped grid. Finally, in the third phase the blocks evolved into a diamond motif.

The earliest of the chief pattern blankets have narrow alternating bands of white and natural black-brown. As time passed there was a consistent broadening of the dark and light stripes, and then symmetrically placed indigo blue stripes came to be included at the center and at each end of the blanket. These first-phase chief pattern blankets have very narrow stripes of bayeta used to delineate the edge between the indigo and the main stripes.

One kind of early chief pattern blanket had very broad indigo stripes without bayeta. They are referred to as the Ute type because it is said that neighboring tribe had a special fondness for the design. A Massacre Cave fragment in the Claflin Collection is of this type and is almost indistinguishable from examples made a half century later.[14]

The design elements of Navajo blankets relate to the body when the blanket is worn. Navajo wearing blankets have two centers, one of which is not apparent when the blanket is viewed as a flat surface. When the blanket is worn, one focal point of the design rests at the center of the back and its counterpart is formed in the front where the two ends are wrapped around the arms and brought forward. The presence of these two focal points was basic to Navajo blanket design, much as the rectangular format, the "illusionary window," was central to European painting.

The second-phase chief pattern blanket is the essence of absolute balance and contained force. It presents a visual confrontation as the dense dark brown stripes contrast with the white stripes. There is no stable foreground and background in this highly conventionalized form. They shift through a planned and controlled structure resulting in sustained tension that grows in intensity with contemplation. The indigo blue stripes are rich and resonant and are defined by the thin bayeta bands.

The Navajos understand the world in terms of energy and change. They are a profoundly musical people whose ceremonies and rituals are sung; and, in the weaving of blankets there were specific chants for each phase of the process. In discussing Navajo weaving an analogy with music and the use of musical terms do not seem artificial or forced. Terms like harmony, counterpoint, theme, and variation apply in particular to the visual impression that the blankets create.

Even in early plain stripe blankets Navajo weaving had an aggressivenss that set it apart from its Pueblo model. The first and second stages of the chief pattern blanket are prime examples. They have a force and color energy that is full and exuber-

1. Chief Pattern Blanket—1st Phase 1850–1860

Although the first phase chief pattern blanket was undoubtedly a dominant style in its day and continued to be woven until the turn of the century, only a handful of examples from the early period remain. The narrowness of the blue and red lines is typical of this style. Early first phase chief pattern blankets reveal the essence of Navajo aesthetics with its paradoxical harmony and aggressiveness. The Maxwell Collection, Maxwell Museum of Anthropology, University of New Mexico, Albuquerque

Length 50 in. (127.0 cm.)
Width 63 in. (160.0 cm.)

		WOOL	DYE
WARP	10/inch	Handspun	None
WEFT			
Blue	27/inch	Handspun	Indigo
Brown	27/inch	Handspun	None
Red	27/inch	3-Ply	Cochineal
Red	27/inch	Unraveled	Cochineal
White	27/inch	Handspun	None

2. Chief Pattern Blanket—Transitional 2nd Phase 1855–1865

In this transitional second phase chief pattern blanket, triangular forms have evolved from the thin stripes of the first phase to break through the stripe areas. These new forms begin to imply what in the third phase becomes the diamond motif. School of American Research Collection in the Museum of New Mexico, Santa Fe

Length 56 in. (142.0 cm.)
Width 70½ in. (179.0 cm.)

		WOOL	DYE
WARP	11/inch	Handspun	None
WEFT			
Blue	35/inch	Handspun	Indigo
Brown	35/inch	Handspun	None
Red	35/inch	Unraveled	Cochineal
White	35/inch	Handspun	None

ant but always under control. There is an individuality in each blanket, a variety and range within a highly defined structure. Although the unique nature of each blanket can be seen within the stripe tradition, it is not as readily apparent here as in the later styles.

The integrity and balance, the "wholeness" of Navajo blanket design is perhaps more remarkable considering the fact that preliminary drawings were never made. In a religious sense it was Spider Woman working through the individual weaver who directed the growth of the blanket, and baby girls were prepared by a special ritual for their future as weavers. In Navajo legend Spider Man said: "Now you know all that I have named for you. It is yours to work with and to use following your own wishes. But from now on when a baby girl is born to your tribe you shall go and find a spider web which is woven at the mouth of some hole; you must take it and rub it on the baby's hand and arm. Thus, when she grows up she will weave, and her fingers and arms will not tire from the weaving."[15]

Perhaps as a result of this spiritual foundation there is none of the coldness of absolute geometry in the making of these blankets. It is, rather, a controlled artistic process, attempted not by single, exceptional individuals who are considered "artists" but by each woman of the tribe. Women wove as their life experience permitted. There were even prohibitions against excessive time spent at the loom: "To overcome the effects of immoderate weaving, the woman sacrificed to her spindle a prayer stick of yucca, precious stones, feathers, tassels of grass, and pollen."[16]

Central to the personal identity of the Navajo was his dress, particularly the wearing blanket. Each blanket gains power with contemplation and reveals the nature of the individual weaver.

The third phase of the chief pattern blanket occurs in the aftermath of the Navajo experience at Bosque Redondo. The blocks, set into the stripes of the second-phase blankets, develop into a characteristic diamond motif in those of the third.

After Bosque Redondo the Navajos settled down, working to re-establish their herds of horses and sheep and other crops and, in general, to begin life again in their own land. They returned to a reservation drastically smaller than their original lands where hogans, herds, orchards, and crops had been systematically destroyed. They could no longer raid to gain wealth or to survive in times of crop failure. With this aggressive mode of life gone, subsistence became more of a struggle for the Navajos, but their daily routine continued much as before.

The late 1860s and early 70s was not a period of great stylistic change in blanket styles. Saxony yarn became more available and began to replace unraveled cloth. Saxony was often combined with bayeta and homsepun yarn in the same blanket. At the same time, bayeta gradually began to be replaced by an American fabric. Known today simply as American flannel, it was generally aniline-dyed and of an orange-red color. Because of its coarseness, the Navajos often respun the resulting yarn before using it.

The 1870s saw the beginning of what would be a continuous contact with the white man. The first trading post was established at Lee's Ferry in 1874, and, although the Navajos were engaged in trading blankets for horses, during the decade the blanket remained primarily an object for their own use rather than for trade.

It is often impossible to distinguish between blankets of the late 1860s and early 70s. The blankets of the 1870s show more and more use of Saxony, and the fine detail of the terraced line evolves into a serrated edge made up of hundreds of little blocks. Eventually this developed into the saw-toothed edge which became a trademark of the 1880s. Also during this decade an increasing number of different design elements appear in the same piece, often floating in the design field rather than linked to one another.

In the 1870s there was still a very high level of technical excellence in weaving, but the shaping of the designs was often looser than before. Among the most significant design developments was the evolution of the third-phase chief pattern blanket.

The development from the inserted red blocks of the second-phase chief pattern to the diamonds of the third is a steady one. The first dated example we know which shows this change from rectangle to diamond is a piece—with very small half diamonds—collected in the 1860s.[17] By the 1870s the chief pattern had developed into a balanced combination of stripes and diamonds. In the third phase there is a central full diamond, sometimes broken by the center stirpe, surrounded by eight triangular elements at the edges. When the blanket is worn, a complete diamond is seen centered on the front and back of the wearer. The third-phase chief pattern blanket represents a successful blending of the diamond motifs of the bayeta serape and the basic stripe of the chief blanket. The strong image produced by this configuration has a dramatic and distinctive impact that has made it among the best-known of Navajo blankets.

In the serape style, much as in the gradually evolving chief pattern blanket, there is a growing emphasis on the size and effect of terraced forms throughout the 1870s. Terracing, which in pre–Bosque Redondo bayeta serapes is a fine detailing of lines, becomes more forceful, with increasingly large steps. The design comes to be less contained by the underlying horizontal grid. The terraced effect also leads to the creation of strong diagonals outlined by the steps and to the boldness of the terraced diamond motif. The serapes of the 1870s are less restrained than the pre–Bosque Redondo bayeta serapes. More aggressive and muscular, they include larger elements that stand out forcefully in the design. Often there is a lessening of the sense of shapes being locked together. A vacant background space surrounding the dominant elements begins to occur, and these voids are now decorated by small floating motifs.

Another characteristic development of the 1870s is the elaboration of the plain-stripe style. Design elements more frequently enter the horizontal bands, at first contained by and then replacing the straight stripe. Although this banded style had occurred earlier, it did not become popular until the 1870s.

The coming of the railroad in 1880 was an event that dramatically increased the rate of change in Navajo life. Trading posts sprang up all along the route as goods could now be brought from the East to the Navajo country with relative ease and Navajo products, in turn, could be shipped to the eastern markets.

Tools, cloth, canned goods, sugar, and tobacco were now available from the traders, and the Navajos were exposed to an array of new products awakening new appetites. While earlier government attempts to instruct the Navajos in the ways of white culture had failed, the relationship that now developed between the Navajos and their local trader was at a personal level understandable within the context of their culture.

In all but the most remote areas of the reservation, the Navajos now knew a white man who was their liaison with the outside world. He represented their interests in dealing with the government, and, while government-appointed agents would come and go, the trader remained. Frequently married to a Navajo, living in the Navajo country, speaking Navajo, he often grew to have a deep understanding and appreciation of their way of life.

The Navajos responded to the traders' efforts and commitment. Along with material goods, the traders showed them new techniques of agriculture and herding. They frequently served as judges in arbitrating disputes and provided medical assistance. Traders also served the Navajo community by relieving the people of the dread necessity of handling and burying the dead.

At first the major trade items for the Navajos were wool and the skins of native wild animals. Blankets continued to be a valuable commodity and were finding their way in growing numbers into the hands of white settlers. As the ranchers, military, and cowboys did not use these blankets for clothing, but

Ash-tish-kel, about 1874; courtesy of Southwest Museum

rather as bed covers or lap robes, many blankets were woven in larger sizes to satisfy these new uses. A whole new class of blankets developed for these groups. They were often more loosely woven and made with less care, but at the same time they showed a fresh exuberance in their design.

Although blankets of fine quality continued to be made, more and more of them were now made quickly for inexpensive sale. The trader's practice of buying blankets by the pound encouraged the production of outrageously poor blankets. Since the wool was never cleaned, occasional examples of these blankets are found with twigs still protruding from poorly spun yarn. Often blankets were weighted with sand to increase their value for sale. Because of the premium on weight, these blankets have come to be known as "pound blankets."

With the invention of aniline dyes in Germany in 1856, a whole new range of colors became available. They were inexpensive and easier to use than natural dyes. The colors they produced were bright and saturate. As their use spread quickly around the world, weaving traditions and color sensibilities changed, and the Navajos, too, responded to these new colors. Although some aniline dyes were in use in the West during the 1860s, traders introduced the new dyes in bulk for the first time in the 1880s and instructed the Indians in their use.

Whereas previously the Navajo palette had been limited to natural wool colors and to the range of soft colors available in Saxony yarns, in practice the expense and rarity of the latter made their extensive use even more uncommon than that of bayeta. As a rule Saxony was only used in fancy blankets or to provide accents. Now, through the use of inexpensive aniline dyes on native homespun wool, a large range of colors was obtained easily. The color intensity of the new dyes rapidly resulted in new design patterns, and the optical effects of the dense, saturate color were employed for dramatic purposes. Of the designs that evolved, the radiating diamond became the primary motif. The serrated edge and the outline were developed to heighten the effect of juxtaposing one intense color against another. It is by no means an exaggeration to call these blankets "eye-dazzlers."

Blankets of this period have always been held in general contempt, and their loose weave has been seen by some as marking the disintegration of Navajo weaving. While in a limited sense this is true, it can also be said that the era of the eye-dazzler was a period of extraordinary expressiveness. With the break from traditional attitudes, many new and vivid images were created. The best of these blankets have an urgency and explosiveness that, in different visual terms, are just as exciting as the classical control of earlier blanket styles. While eye-dazzlers were usually inferior to earlier blankets in technical quality, the new freedom of color, design, and approach often resulted in a jazz-like quality of relaxed improvisation.

As the Navajo culture moved from calm, complete self-confidence to total surrender and domination by a foreign culture, it was not at all surprising to find the emergence in the 1880s of an explosively "expressionistic" style. Whereas earlier the diamond style had been restricted to "fancy" blankets that had a great sense of restraint and control, in the 1880s the diamond became the dominant motif. The irradiating diamond was used to convey a level of energy and agitation that can only be termed expressionist, just as the plain-stripe style conveyed the essence of classical calm.

Eye-dazzler patterns create movement with strong repetition and contrast heightened by extremely animated line and color. Often they produce optical illusions, for instance, the strengthening of the outlined saw-tooth edge, to such an extent that the eye is caught in the visual whirlpool of the surface and is unable to rest on a stable design element. These blankets are perceived as fields of energy and light. Compared to the glowing color radiance of the earlier tradition, they burst forth with an explosive force, a dramatic and powerful change from the subtlety and refinement of the earlier serape style.

At this time machine-spun aniline-dyed yarn became available. This yarn was produced in Germantown, Pennsylvania, which has given its name to all aniline four-ply material used by the Navajos. Germantown yarn was used to produce very finely woven blankets, much as bayeta and Saxony were used in the preceding period.

The uniform quality of Germantown and the fact that it came ready to use—thereby eliminating arduous preparations of the yarn—freed the weaver to devote more time to weaving very detailed patterns. Not only did Germantown yarn make the execution of these patterns practical, it led to the creation of the most intricate designs ever used by the Navajos as well as to variations on all the traditional earlier styles. At this point, encouraged by traders, the practice of copying an earlier blanket style entered Navajo weaving, and there are examples woven in Germantown yarn of every stylistic type with the exception of the plain-stripe style.

The new Germantown styles demonstrated a sense of mechanical precision in both concept and weaving. The irradiating diamond was the most important design innovation. Whereas a pattern previously might have been divided into three or four

3. Stripe 1790–1805

Fragments found in Massacre Cave (1805) are the first known examples of Navajo weaving, and this particular piece is the largest of these fragments. Stripe blankets were made from the earliest times through the 1890s. In fact, this piece is indistinguishable from some dated fifty years later. The Maxwell Collection, Maxwell Museum of Anthropology, University of New Mexico, Albuquerque

Length 48 in. (122.0 cm.)
Width 53 in. (134.5 cm.)

		WOOL	DYE
WARP	4/inch	Handspun	None
WEFT			
Brown	6/inch	Handspun	None
White	6/inch	Handspun	None

4. Chief Pattern Blanket—1st Phase Ute Style 1850–1860

The Ute style is a variation on the format of the first phase chief pattern blanket. But in this type there is a wide center band of indigo blue, without the thin red bayeta stripes. Arizona State Museum, The University of Arizona, Tucson

Length 63¼ in. (161.0 cm.)
Width 75 in. (190.5 cm.)

		WOOL	DYE
WARP	11/inch	Handspun	None
WEFT			
Brown	32/inch	Handspun	None
Blue	32/inch	Handspun	Indigo
White	32/inch	Handspun	None

5. Chief Pattern Blanket—1st Phase Ute Style 1850–1865

Named for the Utes because of the tribe's fondness for it, the style is distinguished by its broad center stripe. The Massacre Cave fragments in the Claflin Collection indicate that this design existed in a smaller scale before 1800. Natural History Museum of Los Angeles County

Length 53½ in. (136.0 cm.)
Width 71½ in. (182.0 cm.)

		WOOL	DYE
WARP	10/inch	Handspun	None
WEFT			
Blue	30/inch	Handspun	Indigo
Brown	30/inch	Handspun	None
White	30/inch	Handspun	None

Navajo man, about 1900; courtesy of History Division, Natural History Museum of Los Angeles County. Photograph by A. C. Vroman

parts as it progressed from the middle of the blanket to the edge, now there were often as many as ten to fifteen main units and, in addition, still smaller motifs enriching the design. The manipulation of Germantown yarn made new visual effects possible. Special variegated yarn, while never as popular as in Mexico, had found a place in Navajo weaving by the 1890s. A particularly painterly effect was obtained by using alternating lines of weft material of contrasting colors.

A few earlier blankets contain small pictographic images, but it was in the 1880s that pictorial representation in Navajo blankets came into general use. Figures of horses, cows, birds, bows and arrows, knives and forks, shovels, pitchforks, houses, and trains began to appear as main design elements.

This was the first break with a long tradition of abstraction, and these images were handled in a way consistent with established design conventions. These blankets never create the illusion of a particular place or of real space; rather, the representational images are used as isolated motifs in the same manner as other design elements. They march in bands within the stripe grid or they appear in the centers of diamonds; rarely does one see them scattered at random in a blanket.

The development of blanket styles in the 1890s is marked by a tendency to place design elements vertically, in contrast to the traditional horizontal emphasis. Stripes, diamonds, zigzags, and rows of stacked triangles crowd the format. Often a lightning-like structure is developed, epitomizing this vertical organization.

The technique called wedge-weave was the forerunner of the new vertical style. This innovation led naturally to the use of zigzag forms by allowing the weft to follow the slanted line of the pattern rather than the traditional horizontal line. Wedge-weave normally results in scalloped edges, as there is no easy way to resolve the borders cleanly. It is often called "pulled-warp" because the warp is drawn from side to side in the weaving process. The wedge-weave technique was uncommon; however, it had a significant aesthetic influence; it was the structural equivalent of the explosive design of the eye-dazzler and a direct antecedent of the vertical designs of the 1890s.

During the 1890s many blankets drawing on traditional designs lacked tension and force. The plastic density of the earlier examples grew out of the weaving process while the designs of the blankets of the 1890s appear applied to the surface from a preconceived plan.

The force and speed with which all of these stylistic and technical changes occurred was remarkable. A Navajo weaver who was fifty years old in 1895 would have been eighteen at the time of the internment at Bosque Redondo and would have lived through all of the major changes of style and technique that we know of in the Navajo blanket tradition.

Regional styles did not begin to develop until the mid-1890s. This is surprising, given the scattered way in which the Navajos lived and their limited means of communication, particularly before Bosque Redondo. While one never finds identical blankets, remarkably similar examples can be found in which subtle differences suggest that they were not woven by the same hand. A careful sorting through thousands of examples will reveal many similar design configurations within each of the styles discussed here. Were they influenced by an innovative weaver? Are they the distinctive work of a single family or clan? Do they represent a regional style? Discussions with experts and a careful study of the literature have produced no real information.

Certainly, the great differences within a single style are linked to the individual nature of each blanket. Some women would have been quick to respond to the latest developments, while the more conservative members of the tribe would have adhered to older motifs. Proximity to the white man, and particularly to the railroad, were factors of major importance. The closer a weaver lived to the railroad, the greater the number of people who might influence her and the more new materials that were available for experimentation. The railroad also increased the possibility of producing blankets solely for trade.

Commercial goods sold by the traders introduced the Navajos to a new set of visual elements—the alphabet. Letters and even whole words began to be incorporated as design motifs into Navajo blankets. They were used as shapes rather than as symbols, and letters were often turned or restructured to resemble established Navajo designs. The letters *E, I, A,* and *W* were similar to traditional motifs, and they were most commonly used. The words that appeared most frequently were those that were printed on supplies offered by the trader.

The early part of the 1890s was the last period in which the Navajos wove blankets for their own use.[18] The traders brought into the territory inexpensive machine-made blankets, particularly the Pendleton Mills products. The establishment of a continuing trade relationship created a constant demand among the Navajos for the goods of the white man. Pendleton blankets were cheaper than native blankets, and the technical skill and energy consumed by blanket-making could now be utilized more profitably by weaving for trade. In view of the close relationship that traditionally existed between the individual Navajo and the blanket he wore, a clear sign of the extent of white influence during these years was that the Navajos would wear machine-made products while devoting their weaving skill to production for trade. That they often followed explicit instructions and wove designs suggested by the trader is further evidence of this change.

The Pendleton was the white man's interpretation of what an Indian blanket should look like. The Pendleton blanket used motifs that were very similar to those of the Navajos. However, these motifs were not used to create any sense of plastic order. Rather, they were arranged in rows like so many decals applied to a beach towel. By the mid-1890s the few wearing blankets still being produced assumed a more printed appearance, similar to that of the Pendleton blankets.

Henceforth, this mechanically drawn and even quality was generally considered desirable in Navajo weaving. When a piece was finished its ultimate use was not determined by the weaver but by the person who bought it. It could be worn by an Indian, used as a bed roll by a cowboy, or thrown on the floor as a rug by a lady in Boston.

While in the 1890s most blankets were becoming quite mechanical and standardized, many were extremely eccentric and unique in concept. This was a period in which the old standards were collapsing, and some weavers, rather than accept the dictates of the trader, utilized the freedom from traditional standards to create works outside the established categories. Certainly the Germantowns represent a high point in terms of technical fineness. Only recently has a handful of weavers at Two Gray Hills surpassed them in a determined, even obsessive, effort to achieve an extremely fine weft count. If one looks at the blankets as works of art rather than as craft objects, beautifully realized design would be considered much more important than the fineness of weaving.

As the railroad transported the blankets from the Southwest, they came into use by people all along its route. A result was that the traders began to influence the Navajos to weave blankets that would find greater acceptance with their eastern clientele. A wearing blanket was not precisely what eastern ladies needed, and by 1900 weavings of various sizes from pillow tops to large rugs were being made. It is unclear when Navajo blankets began to be used as rugs. References do not begin in the Ganado Trading Post files until the late 1890s.[19]

The most dramatic stylistic changes were the popular introduction of the border as a framing device and the limitation of color. While borders did appear in a few very early blankets,[20] they were never commonly used. When they did occur, they were an integral part of the design. The traders urged the use of the border as a device to frame the image. Derived from the oriental rug tradition to which the eastern clientele was accustomed, such a border served to tame the explosiveness of the design. Also at the traders' insistence, color was severely reduced and weaving was done with only the natural colors of the wool. Red was the only exception. Isolated geometric elements began to be placed within the boxed format in a restrained, mundane manner that had more to do with the taste of the new eastern clientele than it did with the choice of the weaver.

Often in these first rugs natural-colored wools were carded and spun together to create a wide variety of tones, from black to white with every shade in between. As a compensation for the loss of color and rhythmic pattern, the random effect of the striated wool was often used to create landscape-like areas which filled in much of the space of the rug, heightened by contrast with the sharp and solid colored borders and design elements. The lazy line that created a definite break in the weaving now came into play as a design element. Randomly striated wool was sharply defined into areas by the lazy lines which created junctures and shifts not unlike the faulting in geologic strata.

Although it is very much our tendency today, it is not quite fair to consider this change from indigenous, individualized art to commercial craft the result of exploitation by the white trader. The Navajos were at this time rebuilding their life style with drastically changed boundaries and limitations, and the prosperity—even the survival—of the tribe depended upon its adaptability. If the transition from blanket to rug marked the end of an art form, it also established a basis for continued economic and social stability. The Navajos' talent for learning from alien cultures while keeping their identity as a people is demonstrated by this transition. Navajo weaving, always valuable to the tribe as a trade resource, became a solid and dependable craft-industry serving a white society far different from customers they had bartered with before. Except for a few discerning private collectors, blankets have been collected by natural history institutions rather than by art musuems. The value of these historical and technical criteria is clear, but we also feel that the viewpoint they imply is severely limited, focusing on only one part of a complex phenomenon.

Navajo captive at Bosque Redondo; courtesy of Arizona Historical Society Library

In visual power and force of statement Navajo blankets represent a high point in the history of American Indian art. The expressive use of color and energy controlled in a two-dimensional surface is remarkable, especially if we consider the great number of fine individual examples that can be found. The general level of quality during the period we have discussed is very high, both in terms of weaving technique and visual expression. Within the tradition the preoccupation with individual creation and artistic choice is even more notable.

Amsden writes of the development of the wearing blanket in the nineteenth century as a process of rapid growth rather than slow evolution of motif and expression. This compressed set of stylistic changes provides a valuable test case in the consideration of artistic change. While we have not attempted to construct a formal apparatus for such a study, we hope that some indications of this approach can be found here. But, the consideration of style in general historical terms is only part of our concern; even more important to us is the experience each blanket offers as a visual statement.

There are still some people who are unable to consider even the greatest of Navajo blankets as beyond the realm of craft because they are woven rather than painted. This cultural bias with regard to both the materials of art and the social role of the artist is contradicted by the Navajo weaving tradition.

In a sense, contemporary artists have led us to a new way of seeing these blankets, one which would not have been readily accessible thirty or more years ago. That a great many of these artists have a serious interest in Navajo blankets is demonstrated by their personal collections. The premises of "abstract art" are no longer controversial, but neither are they deeply rooted in our society. Abstraction was not a special "artist's" vocabulary for the Navajos who wove these blankets; rather, it was a valid means of personal expression in their

6. Chief Pattern Blanket—1st Phase 1850–1860

First phase chief pattern blankets always follow an identical format consisting of contrasting stripes of deep brown-black and creamy white, of indigo blue and cochineal red. This format with its special color proportions, intensities, and sequences is indistinguishable from the effect it produces; what is apprehended is not a collection of parts but a single radiant image. Anthony Berlant, Santa Monica, California

Length 55 in. (139.5 cm.)
Width 69 in. (175.5 cm.)

		WOOL	DYE
WARP	8/inch	Handspun	None
WEFT			
Brown	19/inch	Handspun	None
Blue	19/inch	Handspun	Indigo
Red	19/inch	Unraveled	Cochineal
White	19/inch	Handspun	None

society. The Navajo weaver dealt with many of the same concerns as contemporary artists, but in the more integral Navajo culture these concerns were central and shared by everyone.

Of course, we cannot view these blankets as they were seen by the Navajos who made them. We can get close to their culture but can never fully experience it. Art for the Navajos was not separate from life, and the best blankets show a combination of conscious and subconscious elements, a balance between tradition and improvisation that came to them naturally.

There was a dynamic connection between design and function—a Navajo blanket expressed the character and position of its wearer and gave him a kind of permanent gesture. Blankets when worn in the traditional manner emphasized the strength and verticality of the wearer's posture. They also limited and defined his characteristic movements and stances. While this is true to some degree of almost all dress, the link between abstract design and the affirmation of an individual body is particularly strong and vital here.

The Navajos lived in small isolated family units, and one can imagine the role of the blanket at larger gatherings. The blankets were a form of communication, of direct exchange between members of the tribe, since knowledge and expertise in weaving were shared by all.

There are constants in the Navajo experience which underlie the tradition of these blankets. Foremost of these is a feeling of energy. It is as if each blanket were a diagram of the spiritual presence of an individual. The blankets also present a distillation of the landscape of the Navajo country where the strong sense of horizon and defined field of vision become part of one's perception, as does color used in powerful and controlled patterns of contrast and confluence.

A tradition always seems more undifferentiated when it is not something we take for granted. One can think in general of all Italian High Renaissance Madonnas as similar in many respects, but one need only look at the paintings of such artists as Bellini, Raphael, and DaVinci to observe strong individual differences within a given tradition.

It is customarily thought that the personality of the creator is somehow less present in tribal art than the art of our own culture, but in fact our fascination with Navajo weaving has been in experiencing the sense of the individual through the work, in seeing how in each instance the convention is handled in a unique way.

This is a selection of the work of eighty-one women artists. While the Navajos learned the craft of weaving from the Pueblos, in Pueblo society men have always been the weavers. In fact, in most cultures textiles have been made by men who were part of a specific professional class of weavers. For the Navajos, weaving was not a separate profession—it was part of the cycle of life for the Navajo woman. This widespread practice of weaving did not lead to mediocre amateurism; rather, it became an important aspect of a society in which every woman functioned as an artist. The blankets have a dynamic force and consistently aggressive quality which our culture has not considered a feminine trait. The creative independence, within the blanket tradition, points to important freedoms of women in Navajo society. In this matriarchal society property, for example, was owned in the woman's name, and the family line was traced through the woman.

The last few years have seen a rapid growth of interest in the American Indian. A study of Indian culture reveals an American history of great antiquity and profundity. The Navajo blanket gives us a feeling of this time and place and a vision of the world that can never be ours directly.

The bold, visual presence of Navajo blankets is immediately perceived. An interest in their specific history develops from a first encounter. One might think of a blanket as an Indian rug, then as a Navajo chief pattern blanket, and finally as a second-phase bayeta chief pattern blanket of about 1865. Ultimately the focus upon the distinct qualities of each blanket reveals the sensibility of an individual artist and the spirit of a people.

7. Chief Pattern Blanket—2nd Phase 1850–1865

First and second phase chief pattern blankets were made adhering to the same basic format, with only slight variations introduced. Their color and proportion obviously represented an ideal for the Navajo weaver. Lowe Art Museum, Alfred I. Barton Collection, Coral Gables, Florida

Length 49 in. (124.0 cm.)
Width 69 in. (175.5 cm.)

		WOOL	DYE
WARP	9/inch	Handspun	None
WEFT			
Blue	23/inch	Handspun	Indigo
Brown	23/inch	Handspun	None
Red	27/inch	Unraveled	Cochineal
White	23/inch	Handspun	None

8. Chief Pattern Blanket—2nd Phase 1850–1865

In the second phase chief pattern blanket the basic design format has evolved from the first phase with the development of blocks out of the red stripes. Natural History Museum of Los Angeles County

Length 57 in. (145.0 cm.)
Width 71 in. (178.0 cm.)

		WOOL	DYE
WARP	9/inch	Handspun	None
WEFT			
Brown	25/inch	Handspun	None
Blue	25/inch	Handspun	Indigo
Green-Blue	25/inch	Handspun	Indigo + Native
Red	27/inch	Unraveled	Cochineal
White	25/inch	Handspun	None

9. Chief Pattern Blanket—2nd Phase 1860–1870

Representing a slightly later development within the second phase chief pattern format, the blocks of this blanket are no longer connected by red lines. William H. Claflin, Boston

Length 56 in. (192.0 cm.)
Width 69½ in. (176.5 cm.)

		WOOL	DYE
WARP	12/inch	Handspun	None
WEFT			
Blue	40/inch	Handspun	Indigo
Brown	40/inch	Handspun	None
Red	40/inch	Unraveled	Cochineal
White	40/inch	Handspun	None

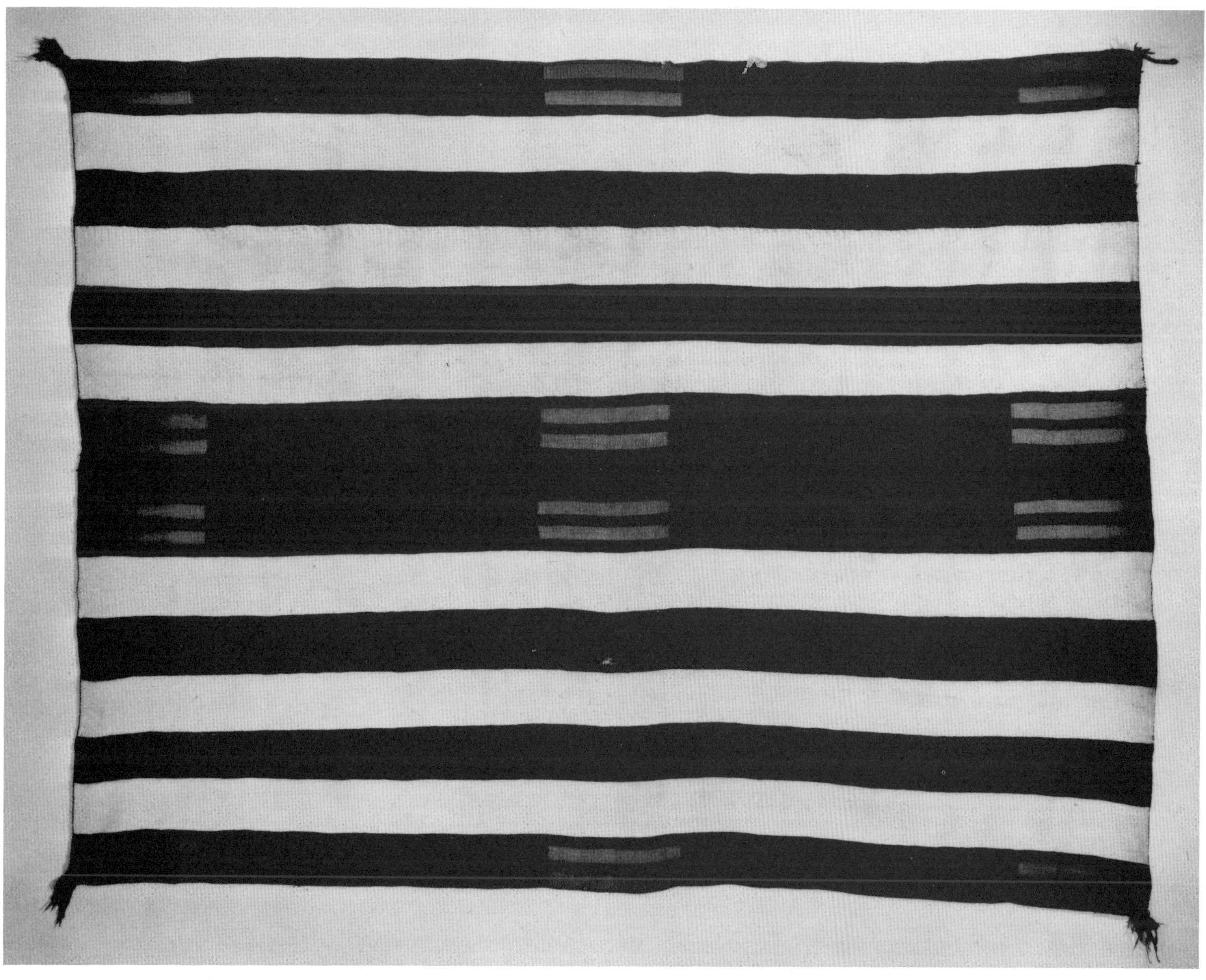

10. Woman's Blanket 1865–1875

This woman's blanket parallels the man's first phase chief pattern blanket with respect to design configuration. It differs, however, from the man's in its narrower stripes. These stripes are of various natural light browns except in early examples where they are white and black-brown. The American Museum of Natural History, New York

Length 43 in. (109.0 cm.)
Width 58 in. (147.0 cm.)

		WOOL	DYE
WARP	8/inch	Handspun	None
WEFT			
Black	17/inch	Handspun	Native
Brown	17/inch	Handspun	None
Blue	22/inch	Handspun	Indigo
Red	22/inch	3-Ply	Cochineal

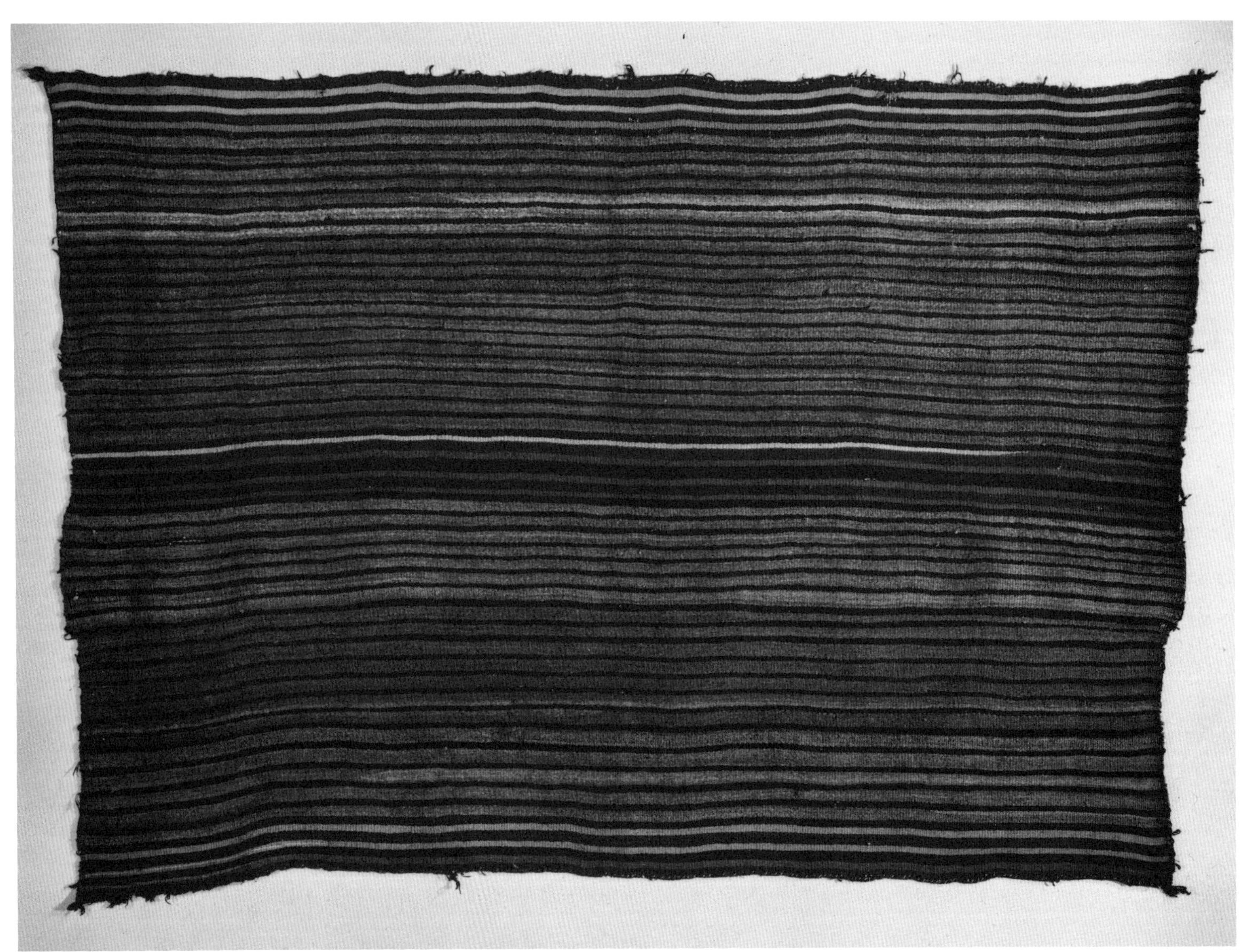

11. Serape Style 1850–1865

This blanket is particularly striking for the expansive quality of its design. Contributing to the sense of great size is the lack of central diamonds and the almost completely uninterrupted area of blue and white. Natural History Museum of Los Angeles County

Length 84 in. (213.5 cm.)
Width 59 in. (150.0 cm.)

		WOOL	DYE
WARP	12/inch	Handspun	None
WEFT			
Blue	21/inch	Handspun	Indigo
Red	21/inch	Unraveled	Cochineal
White	21/inch	Handspun	None

12. Serape Style 1840–1860

The complex structure of this blanket is masterful in its virtuosity and control. Southwest Museum, Los Angeles

Length 68 1/2 in. (174.0 cm.)
Width 50 in. (127.0 cm.)

		WOOL	DYE
WARP	12/inch	Handspun	None
WEFT			
Blue	39/inch	Handspun	Indigo
Red	39/inch	Unraveled	Cochineal
White	39/inch	Handspun	None

13. Serape Style 1850–1865

This delicate blanket is strongly reminiscent of Rio Grande blankets made by the Spanish New Mexican settlers of the same period. The similarity is most apparent in the scale of the central interlocking diamonds and in the general color tone. Lowe Art Museum, Alfred I. Barton Collection, Coral Gables, Florida

Length 59 1/2 in. (150.0 cm.)
Width 42 1/4 in. (107.0 cm.)

		WOOL	DYE
WARP	12/inch	Handspun	None
WEFT			
Black	24/inch	Handspun	Native
Blue	24/inch	Handspun	Indigo
Green	24/inch	Unraveled	Native
Red	24/inch	Unraveled	Cochineal
Red	24/inch	3-Ply	Cochineal
White	24/inch	Handspun	None

14. Serape Style 1850–1860

Originally collected by the Spiegelbergs, one of the first merchant families to settle in Santa Fe, this blanket subsequently became part of the Indian Department Collection of the Fred Harvey Company. Herman Schweizer, who headed the department, considered this to be the finest blanket he collected. Lowe Art Museum, Alfred I. Barton Collection, Coral Gables, Florida

Length 83 in. (211.0 cm.)
Width 57½ in. (146.0 cm.)

		WOOL	DYE
WARP	11/inch	Handspun	None
WEFT			
Blue	26/inch	Handspun	Indigo
Light Blue	26/inch	Handspun	Indigo
Red	26/inch	Unraveled	Cochineal
White	26/inch	Handspun	None

15. Chief Pattern, 2nd Phase, Woman's Type 1860–1870

Intense green lines of fine handspun wool spark the complementary red zones in which they occur. The thinness and irregularity of the brown-black lines create a shimmering effect. School of American Research Collection in the Museum of New Mexico, Santa Fe

Length $35^{3}/_{4}$ in. (90.5 cm.)
Width 52 in. (132.0 cm.)

		WOOL	DYE
WARP	9/inch	Handspun	None
WEFT			
Blue	18/inch	Handspun	Indigo
Brown	18/inch	Handspun	None
Green	18/inch	Handspun	Native
Red	18/inch	Unraveled	Cochineal
White	18/inch	Unraveled	None

16. Serape Style 1850–1865

The rectangular block pattern and the dominant green color are most unusual in blankets of this period. Complementing the delicate green color is the combination of smooth Saxony yarn matched with the fine handspun yarn. Arizona State Museum, The University of Arizona, Tucson

Length $77\frac{1}{2}$ in. (197.0 cm.)
Width 51 in. (129.5 cm.)

		WOOL	DYE
WARP	12/inch	Handspun	None
WEFT			
Blue	29/inch	Handspun	Indigo
Green	29/inch	Unraveled	Natural
Pink	29/inch	3-Ply	Natural
Red	29/inch	Unraveled	Natural
Dark Red	29/inch	Unraveled	Cochineal
Yellow	29/inch	3-Ply	Natural
White	29/inch	3-Ply	Natural
White	29/inch	Handspun	None

17. Serape Style 1850–1860

The diamond and the stripe are the basic design elements of the serape style. In this example, unlike most others, the diamonds are linked together to create a weblike overlay. William H. Claflin, Boston

Length 68 in. (173.0 cm.)
Width $47^{1}/_{2}$ in. (120.5 cm.)

		WOOL	DYE
WARP	15/inch	Handspun	None
WEFT			
Blue	40/inch	Handspun	Indigo
Red	40/inch	3-Ply	Cochineal
White	40/inch	Handspun	None

18. Serape Style 1850–1860

Both the finely stepped edge and the use of stripes to build designs occur in blankets of this early period. The detail shows three-ply saxony yarn in the background and in the pale stripes; it is smooth and silky in texture. Arizona State Museum, The University of Arizona, Tucson

Length $65^{1}/_{4}$ in. (166.5 cm.)
Width 45 in. (114.2 cm.)

		WOOL	DYE
WARP	10/inch	Handspun	None
WEFT			
Blue	24/inch	Handspun	Indigo
Green	24/inch	3-Ply	Native
Red	24/inch	3-Ply	Cochineal
White	32/inch	Handspun	None

1
MADE IN U.S.A.
2
3
4
5
6
7

19. Poncho 1850–1860

This poncho has an unusually jammed and muscular quality to the drawing. The center third of the blanket is a radiating diamond pattern in which element echoes element symmetrically. At each end the alignment shifts, producing a powerful visual disruption. The University Museum, University of Pennsylvania, Philadelphia

Length 70 in. (178.0 cm.)
Width $57^{1}/_{2}$ in. (146.0 cm.)

		WOOL	DYE
WARP	11/inch	Handspun	None
WEFT			
Blue	30/inch	Handspun	Indigo
Red	30/inch	Unraveled	?
White	30/inch	Handspun	None

20. Poncho 1865–1875

This unique blanket has the quality of a sampler for it incorporates almost every traditional Navajo motif, including an early use of figurative elements. Natural History Museum of Los Angeles County

Length $87^{1}/_{2}$ in. (222.0 cm.)
Width 50 in. (127.0 cm.)

		WOOL	DYE
WARP	11/inch	Handspun	None
WEFT			
Brown-Green (faded)	22/inch	Unraveled	Aniline
Blue	20/inch	Homespun	Indigo
Blue-Green (faded)	22/inch	Unraveled	Aniline
Grey (faded violet)	22/inch	Unraveled	Aniline
Red (various shades)	22/inch	Unraveled	?
White	20/inch	Homespun	None

21. Stripe Child's Blanket 1850–1860

This child's blanket with its subtle handling of detail, scale, and tone reveals the degree of refinement reached within the stripe tradition. The Heard Museum, Phoenix

Length 51 3/4 in. (131.5 cm.)
Width 32 1/4 in. (82.0 cm.)

		WOOL	DYE
WARP	40/inch	Handspun	None
WEFT			
Blue	46/inch	Handspun	Indigo
Red	46/inch	Unraveled	Cochineal
White	40/inch	Handspun	None

22. Woman's Dress 1850–1865

Only in the woman's dress does one find large areas of solid color. In this example the variations in the natural browns show the structure of the weaving and at the same time suggest the topography of the Navajo landscape. The Denver Art Museum Native Arts Collection

Lengths $49^{1}/_{2}$ in. (125.7 cm.)
49 in. (124.5 cm.)
Widths $33^{1}/_{4}$ in. (84.5 cm.)
34 in. (86.5 cm.)

		WOOL	DYE
WARP	13/inch	Handspun	None
WEFT			
Brown	24/inch	Handspun	None
Blue	32/inch	Handspun	Indigo
Red	38/inch	Unraveled	Cochineal

23. Woman's Dress 1855–1865

The style of the woman's dress was more conventionalized than that of the blanket and changed very little throughout the nineteenth century. Usually it contained the finest of materials and was extraordinarily well made. Anthony Berlant, Santa Monica, California

Lengths 52 1/4 in. (132.5 cm.)
51 1/2 in. (130.5 cm.)
Widths 32 in. (81.0 cm.)
35 in. (89.0 cm.)

		WOOL	DYE
WARP	10/inch	Handspun	None
WEFT			
Blue	29/inch	Handspun	Indigo
Brown	29/inch	Handspun	None
Red	29/inch	Unraveled	Cochineal

24. Chief Pattern Blanket—2nd Phase 1860–1870

Characteristic of later second phase chief pattern blankets is the appearance of small design elements within the blocks. Anthony Berlant, Santa Monica, California

Length 55 in. (139.5 cm.)
Width 69 in. (175.5 cm.)

		WOOL	DYE
WARP	10/inch	Handspun	None
WEFT			
Black	37/inch	Handspun	Native
Blue	37/inch	Handspun	Indigo
Brown	37/inch	Handspun	None
Green	37/inch	3-Ply	Natural
Red	37/inch	3-Ply	Cochineal
Red	37/inch	Unraveled	Cochineal
White	37/inch	Handspun	None

25. Stripe 1850–1870

The plain stripe blanket was a common style until the 1890s. This example is similar in the color and handling of stripes to the Massacre Cave fragment dated before 1805 (plate 3). Anthony Berlant, Santa Monica, California.

Length 74 in. (188.0 cm.)
Width 62 in. (167.5 cm.)

		WOOL	DYE
WARP	6/inch	Handspun	None
WEFT			
Brown	9/inch	Handspun	None
Blue	9/inch	Handspun	Indigo
White	9/inch	Handspun	None

26. Stripe 1840–1870

The stripe blanket is based on the Pueblo tradition. Frequently it is unclear whether a blanket is Pueblo or Navajo. It is generally believed that only the Navajo blankets utilize lazy lines and three strand wrapped edges; however, historical evidence shows that these points are not absolute criteria. Anthony Berlant, Santa Monica, California

Length 80½ in. (204.5 cm.)
Width 53 in. (134.0 cm.)

		WOOL	DYE
WARP	7/inch	Handspun	None
WEFT			
Brown	13/inch	Handspun	None
Blue	13/inch	Handspun	Indigo
Red	13/inch	Unraveled	Cochineal
White	13/inch	Handspun	None

27. Child's Blanket   1855–1870

The very simple format of this blanket is set off by the refinement of its details: the extraordinary control of rhythms, scale, and balance, and the jewel-like radiance of the color complements.   School of American Research Collection in the Museum of New Mexico, Santa Fe

Length $49\frac{1}{2}$ in. (125.5 cm.)
Width 35 in. (89.0 cm.)

		WOOL	DYE
WARP	12/inch	Handspun	None
WEFT			
Blue	12/inch	Handspun	Indigo
Green	12/inch	Unraveled	Natural
Yellow-Green	12/inch	Unraveled	Natural
Red	12/inch	Unraveled	Cochineal
Red	12/inch	3-Ply	Cochineal
White	48/inch	Unraveled	None

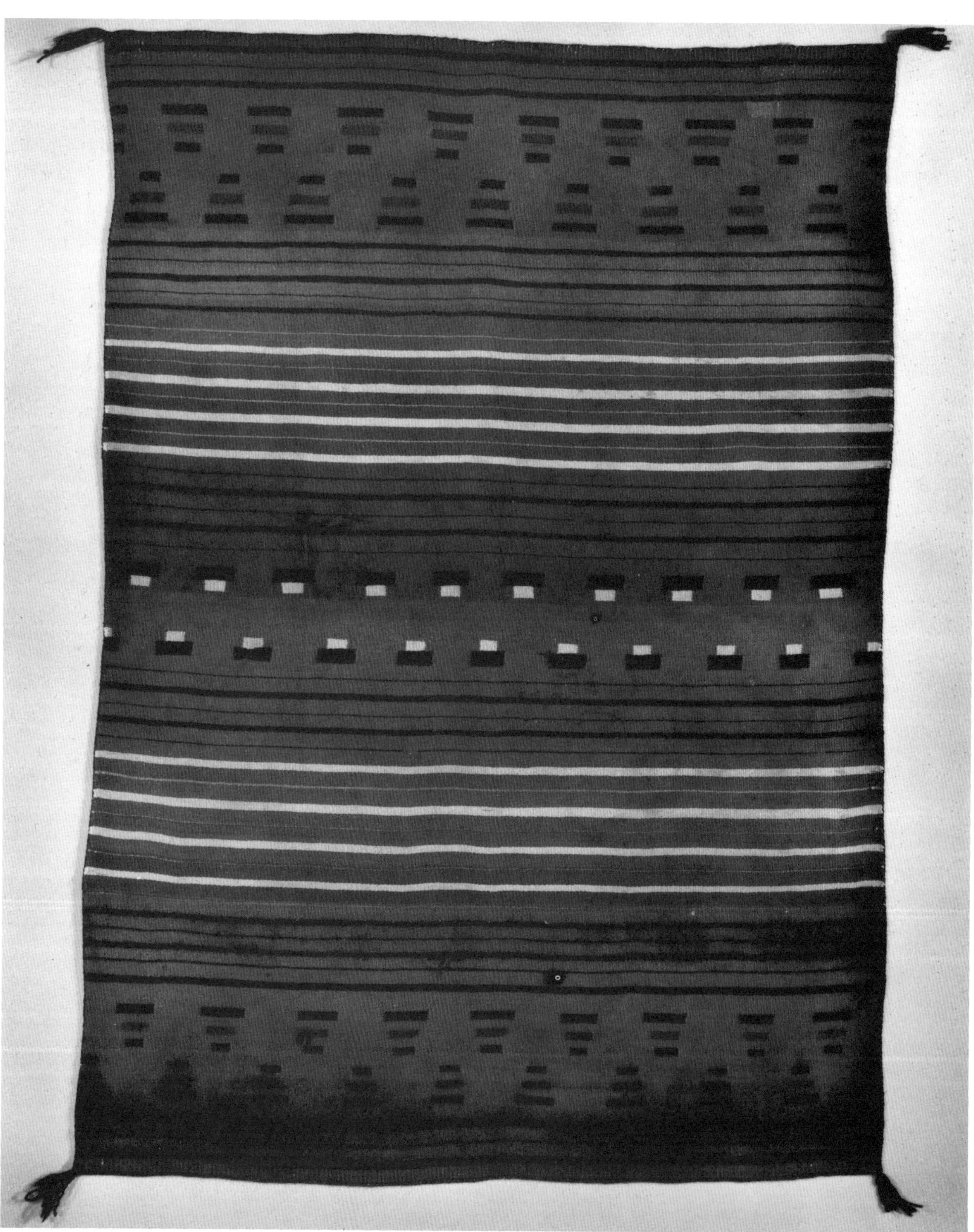

28. Serape Style 1860–1870

Amsden notes on a tag attached to this blanket that at the end of the early serape period the diamond motif evolves into undulating lines. Southwest Museum, Los Angeles

Length 72 in. (185.0 cm.)
Width 52 in. (132.0 cm.)

		WOOL	DYE
WARP	10/inch	Handspun	None
WEFT			
Blue	27/inch	Handspun	Indigo
Red	27/inch	Unraveled	Cochineal
White	27/inch	Handspun	None

29. Chief Pattern Blanket—3rd Phase 1865–1870

When during a game of Indian poker in 1871 Marianno (pictured opposite), a war chief under Chief Manuelita, "was broke and wanted a stake to play more," he sold this blanket to J. B. Givens. Navajo Tribal Museum, Window Rock, Arizona. Photo by Ben Wittick, Collections of the Museum of New Mexico.

Length 58 in. (147.0 cm.)
Width 71 in. (180.5 cm.)

		WOOL	DYE
WARP	12/inch	Handspun	None
WEFT			
Brown	40/inch	Handspun	None
Blue	40/inch	Handspun	Indigo
Red	40/inch	Unraveled	Cochineal
White	40/inch	Handspun	None

Wittick Photo
05 Mariano
Navajo Chief
New Mexico

30. Chief Pattern Blanket—3rd Phase 1868–1875

Often a slight variation in a traditional pattern creates a unique effect. In this chief pattern blanket the corner motifs are not filled in, allowing the stripes to continue to the ends. This variation produces the sensation that the diamond elements float above the stripes. Museum of Navajo Ceremonial Art, Inc., Santa Fe

Length 73½ in. (187.0 cm.)
Width 56 in. (142.0 cm.)

		WOOL	DYE
WARP	12/inch	Handspun	None
WEFT			
Brown	24/inch	Handspun	None
Blue	24/inch	Handspun	Indigo
Red	24/inch	Unraveled or "Bayeta Thread" 1-Ply	Cochineal
White	24/inch	Handspun	None

31. Late Serape Style 1865–1875

Striking in both composition and color, this blanket produces a feeling of great open space. The stepped edges of the mid-1860s here evolve into lines composed of tiny blocks. Anthony Berlant, Santa Monica, California

Length $73^{1}/_{2}$ in. (187.0 cm.)
Width 56 in. (142.0 cm.)

		WOOL	DYE
WARP	10/inch	Handspun	None
WEFT			
Blue	31/inch	Handspun	Indigo
Green	31/inch	3-Ply	?
Red	31/inch	3-Ply	Cochineal
Light Red	31/inch	3-Ply	?
Orange	31/inch	3-Ply	?

32. Stripe 1870–1880

In this blanket one finds the rare combination of natural cochineal and aniline red dyed yarns. The multiplicity of colors in the stripe areas produces bands of unusual richness, and the effect of these bands is heightened by the contrast with the cool natural whites. Thomas Woodard, Gallup, New Mexico

Length 71 1/4 in. (181.5 cm.)
Width 54 1/2 in. (138.0 cm.)

		WOOL	DYE
WARP	9/inch	Handspun	None
WEFT			
Blue	16/inch	Handspun	Indigo
Brown	16/inch	Handspun	None
Green	16/inch	Handspun	?
Red	16/inch	Unraveled	Cochineal
Red	28/inch	3-Ply	?
Orange-Red	16/inch	3-Ply	Aniline
White	20/inch	Handspun	None
Yellow	16/inch	Handspun	?

33. Late Serape Style 1865–1875

A sense of the Navajo landscape is particularly strong in this example.
William H. Claflin, Boston

Length 71 in. (185.5 cm.)
Width 47 in. (119.5 cm.)

		WOOL	DYE
WARP	8/inch	Handspun	None
WEFT			
Blue	20/inch	Handspun	Indigo
Light Blue	20/inch	Handspun	Indigo
Red	20/inch	Recarded	Cochineal
White	20/inch	Handspun	None

34. Late Serape Style 1865–1875

An atypical variation of the serape style, this blanket has an underlying banded structure and a muted pastel color range. Lowe Art Museum, Alfred I. Barton Collection, Coral Gables, Florida

Length 83 in. (211.0 cm.)
Width 57 1/2 in. (146.0 cm.)

		WOOL	DYE
WARP	11/inch	Handspun	None
WEFT			
Beige	26/inch	3-Ply	Aniline
Blue	26/inch	3-Ply Unraveled	?
Green	26/inch	3-Ply	Aniline
Red	26/inch	3-Ply	?
Red	26/inch	1-Ply	?
Violet	26/inch	3-Ply	Aniline
White	26/inch	3-Ply + Unraveled	None

35. Terraced 1870–1875

Strong angular and softer sloping lines are contrasted in this late bayeta period serape. The feather-like projections emerging from the sloping lines are used to create an illusion of roundness and undulation. Particularly interesting is the scale; design elements are much larger than usual. The American Museum of Natural History, New York

Length 68 in. (173.0 cm.)
Width $52^{1}/_{2}$ in. (133.0 cm.)

		WOOL	DYE
WARP	12/inch	Handspun	None
WEFT			
Blue	31/inch	Handspun	Indigo
Red	31/inch	Unraveled	Cochineal
White	31/inch	Handspun	None

36. Late Serape Style 1870–1880

Both the vertical design and the technique of diagonal weaving are precursors of the wedge-weave style which developed in the 1880s. In the detail one can see the contrast between the unraveled bayeta yarn in the center and the zig-zag stripes of handspun yarn at the sides. The bayeta yarn has a scratchier texture. Frequently it has a speckled quality resulting from the fact that the original bayeta fabric was dyed after it was woven. Natural History Museum of Los Angeles County

Length 80 in. (203.0 cm.)
Width 52 in. (132.0 cm.)

		WOOL	DYE
WARP	8/inch	Handspun	None
WEFT			
Blue	18/inch	Handspun	Indigo
Red	18/inch	Unraveled	Cochineal
Pink	18/inch	3-Ply	?
White	18/inch	Handspun	None

37. Serape Style—Terraced 1865–1875

This blanket was collected by an agent of the Ute Reservation in Colorado in the mid-1870s. Referring to it, Amsden noted, "The breakdown of the flowing terraced figure into single units is an interesting feature of this specimen and a sign of the times."[21] William H. Claflin, Boston

Length 67 in. (170.5 cm.)
Width 52 in. (132.0 cm.)

		WOOL	DYE
WARP	9/inch	Handspun	None
WEFT			
Blue	23/inch	Handspun	Indigo
Light Blue	23/inch	Handspun	Indigo
Red	23/inch	Unraveled	Cochineal
White	23/inch	Handspun	None

38. Late Serape Style 1868–1880

The dark indigo blue and natural dark brown stripes of this blanket are generally believed to have come from the Hopi tradition. The development of a diamond design over the stripe background occurs in the seventies, as does the use of American flannel, an unraveled orange-red aniline dyed fabric. Anthony Berlant, Santa Monica, California

Length 76 in. (190.5 cm.)
Width $50^{1}/_{2}$ in. (128.0 cm.)

		WOOL	DYE
WARP	7/inch	Handspun	None
WEFT			
Brown	28/inch	Handspun	None
Blue	28/inch	Handspun	Indigo
Red	28/inch	Unraveled	Aniline
White	28/inch	Handspun	None

39. Banded 1865–1875

It is a common misconception that before the advent of aniline dyes, indigenous dyes were used. In fact, the two most common dye colors which preceded aniline dyes, blue and red, came from Mexico. It is unusual to find such an extensive use of native dyes (the yellow and green) as occur in this example. Natural History Museum of Los Angeles County

Length $78^1/_2$ in. (194.5 cm.)
Width $50^1/_2$ in. (128.0 cm.)

		WOOL	DYE
WARP	10/inch	Handspun	None
WEFT			
Brown	20/inch	Handspun	None
Blue	20/inch	Handspun	Indigo
Green	20/inch	Handspun	Indigo and Native
White	20/inch	Handspun	None
Yellow	20/inch	Handspun	Native

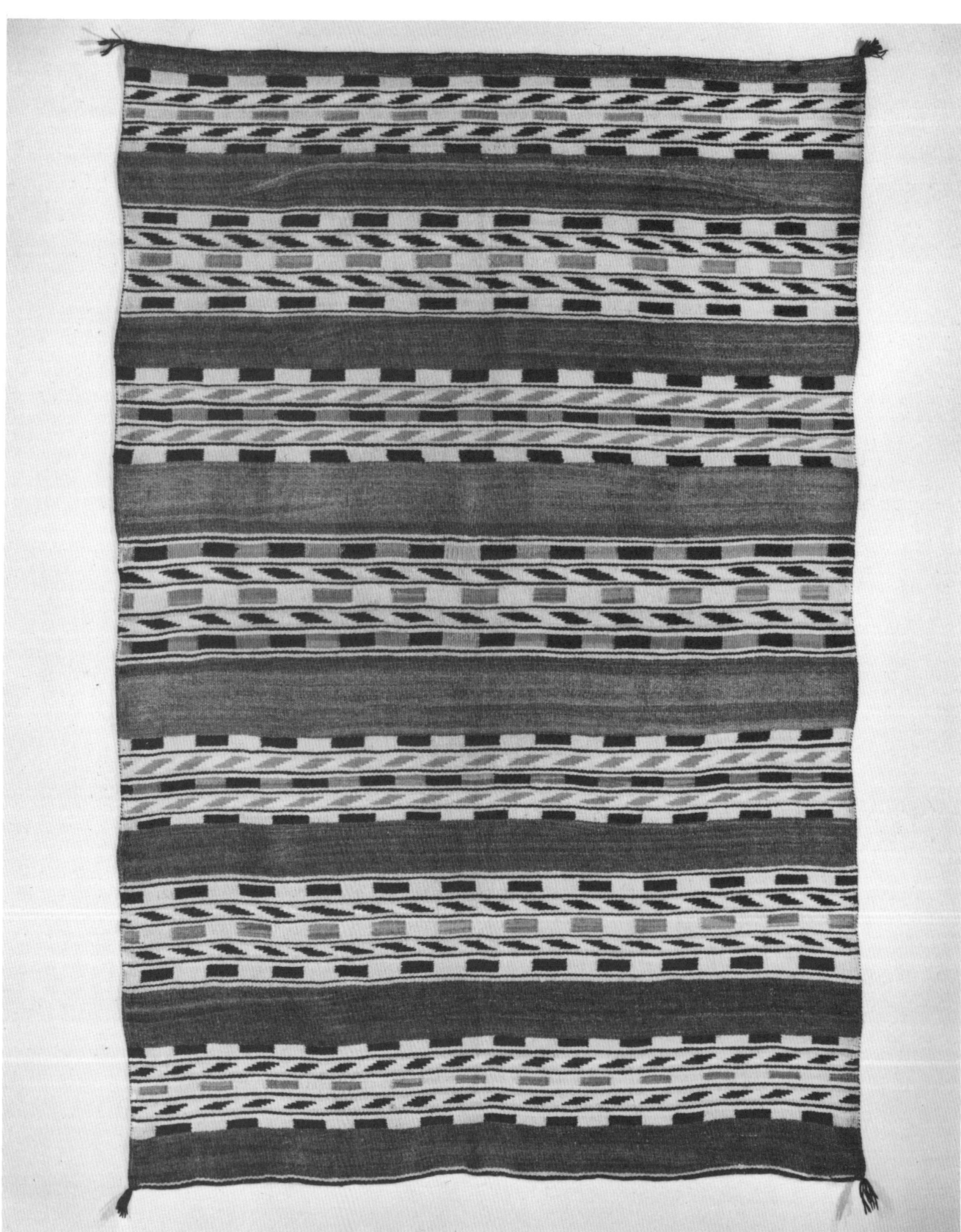

40. Late Serape Style 1870–1875

It is rare to find specific information either about the dating of Navajo blankets or about the circumstances surrounding their collection. W. H. Claflin, who recorded all available information about the blankets he collected, states that this blanket was originally collected by Miss Eliza Hosmer during the 1870s while she served as a teacher in the Romona (Indian) School in Santa Fe. William H. Claflin, Boston

Length 79½ in. (202.0 cm.)
Width 51 in. (129.5 cm.)

		WOOL	DYE
WARP	13/inch	Handspun	None
WEFT			
Blue	31/inch	Handspun	Indigo
Green	31/inch	Unraveled	Native
Red	31/inch	Unraveled	Cochineal
White	31/inch	Handspun	None

41. Child's Blanket 1855–1870

The type of small weft stripe found in this example is rarely seen except in early blankets. The alternation of such narrow stripes causes the eye to mix the juxtaposed colors, producing a more vibrant color area than would be created by a solid grey. Natural History Museum of Los Angeles County

Length 50 in. (127.0 cm.)
Width 33 in. (84.0 cm.)

		WOOL	DYE
WARP	10/inch	Handspun	None
WEFT			
Brown	20/inch	Handspun	None
Dark Blue	20/inch	Handspun	Indigo
Light Blue	20/inch	Handspun	Indigo
Red	20/inch	Unraveled	Cochineal
Light Red	20/inch	Unraveled	Cochineal
White	20/inch	Handspun	None

42. Late Serape Style 1870–1880

Two features make this unusual among Navajo blankets: a stable background plane—the red field—and the square shape. The fractured diamond lattice work which dominates the blanket can be perceived either as a continuous network or as a series of interlocking larger diamonds. School of American Research Collection in the Museum of New Mexico, Santa Fe

Length $67^{1}/_{2}$ in. (171.5 cm.)
Width $60^{1}/_{2}$ in. (154.0 cm.)

		WOOL	DYE
WARP	13/inch	Handspun	None
WEFT			
Blue	24/inch	Handspun	Indigo
Red	26/inch	3-Ply	?
White	24/inch	Handspun	None

43. Stripe 1870–1880

The simple plain stripe motif of the Pueblo tradition produces a highly complex and subtle effect. Variation in the treatment of the stripes, a lack of parallelism, differences in their widths, delicate and bold color contrast, all assume a more radiant and assertive quality in Navajo hands. Millicent A. Rogers Memorial Museum, Inc., Taos, New Mexico

Length 76 in. (193.0 cm.)
Width 53½ in. (135.5 cm.)

		WOOL	DYE
WARP	8/inch	Handspun	None
WEFT			
Brown	18/inch	Handspun	None
Blue	18/inch	Handspun	Indigo
Red	18/inch	Unraveled	Aniline
Yellow	18/inch	Handspun	?

44. Stripe 1870–1880

The stripes of this blanket are alternately calm and electrically charged.
Millicent A. Rogers Memorial Museum, Inc., Taos, New Mexico

Length $75^1/_2$ in. (192.0 cm.)
Width 49 in. (124.5 cm.)

		WOOL	DYE
WARP	7/inch	Handspun	None
WEFT			
Brown	12/inch	Handspun	None
Blue	14/inch	Handspun	Indigo
Red	24/inch	3-Ply	Cochineal
Red	24/inch	Unraveled	Cochineal
White	28/inch	Handspun	None

45. Banded Style 1865–1875

The serrated zig-zag pinetree-like motif which dominates this blanket and the small split diamonds are typical of the late 1860s and early 1870s. Lowe Art Museum, Alfred I. Barton Collection, Coral Gables, Florida

Length $72^1/_2$ in. (184.5 cm.)
Width 50 in. (126.5 cm.)

		WOOL	DYE
WARP	11/inch	Handspun	None
WEFT			
Blue	25/inch	Handspun	Indigo
Green-Blue	25/inch	Handspun	Indigo & Native
Grey	25/inch	Handspun	None
Red	29/inch	Unraveled	?
Red	29/inch	3-Ply	Cochineal
White	25/inch	Handspun	None
Yellow	25/inch	Handspun	Native

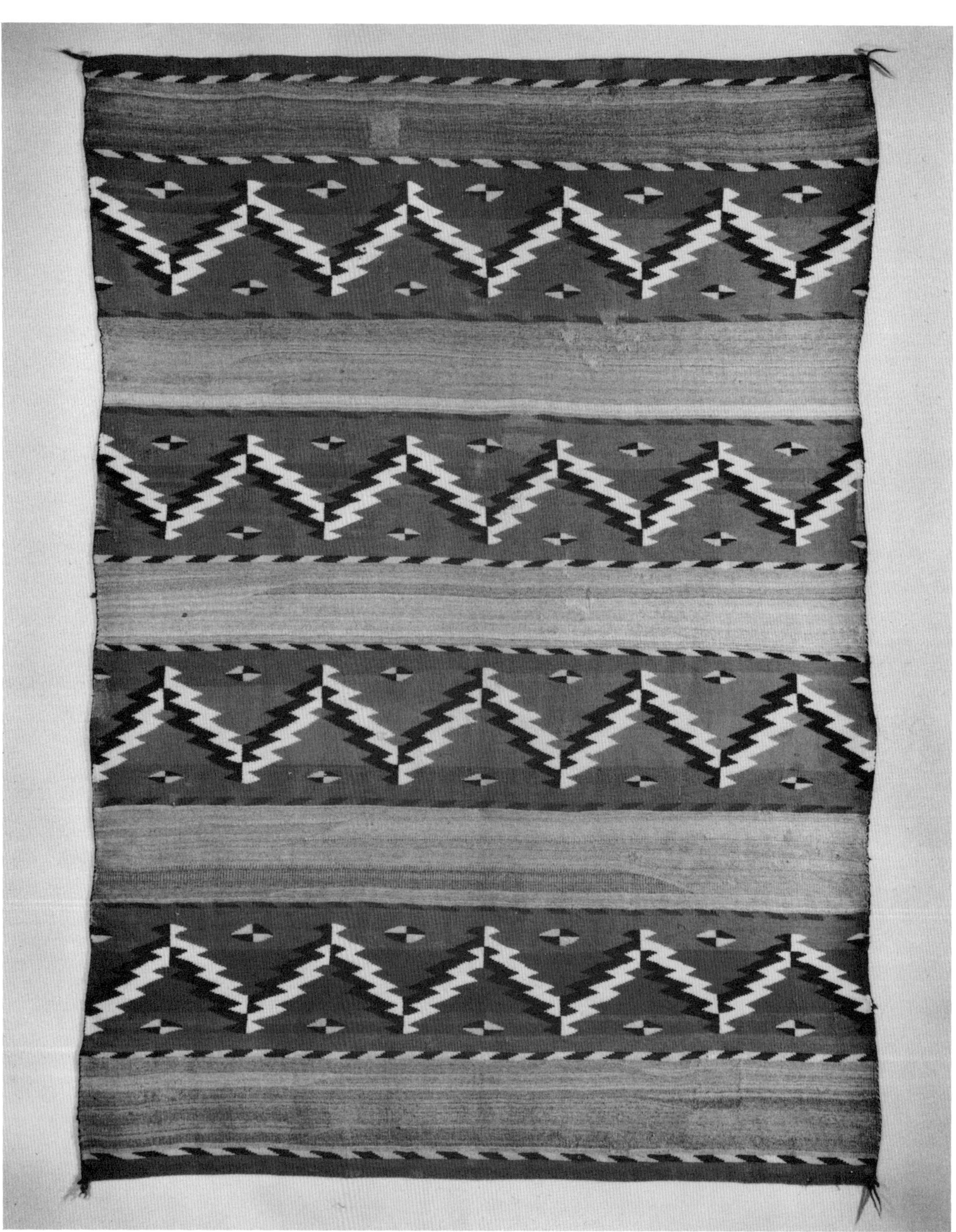

46. Child's Blanket or Saddle Throw 1865–1875

Despite the similarities of motif in this blanket and the one opposite, the change in color and scale produces a quite different effect in each. Byron Harvey, Phoenix, Arizona

Length 45 in. (114.0 cm.)
Width 31 in. (78.5 cm.)

		WOOL	DYE
WARP	15/inch	Handspun	None
WEFT			
Blue	20/inch	Handspun	None
Green	20/inch	Handspun	None
Red	22/inch	Unraveled	?
Red (light)	22/inch	Unraveled	Cochineal
Yellow	20/inch	Handspun	Native

47. Child's Blanket 1870–1880

A vibrating sensation is created by a highly calculated design showing great restraint and control in the variation of each individual zig-zag motif and careful manipulation of the overlapping points. The Heard Museum, Phoenix

Length 53 in. (134.5 cm.)
Width $34^{1}/_{2}$ in. (87.0 cm.)

		WOOL	DYE
WARP	12/inch	Handspun	None
WEFT			
Blue	30/inch	Handspun	Indigo
Red	30/inch	Handspun	?
White	30/inch	Handspun	None

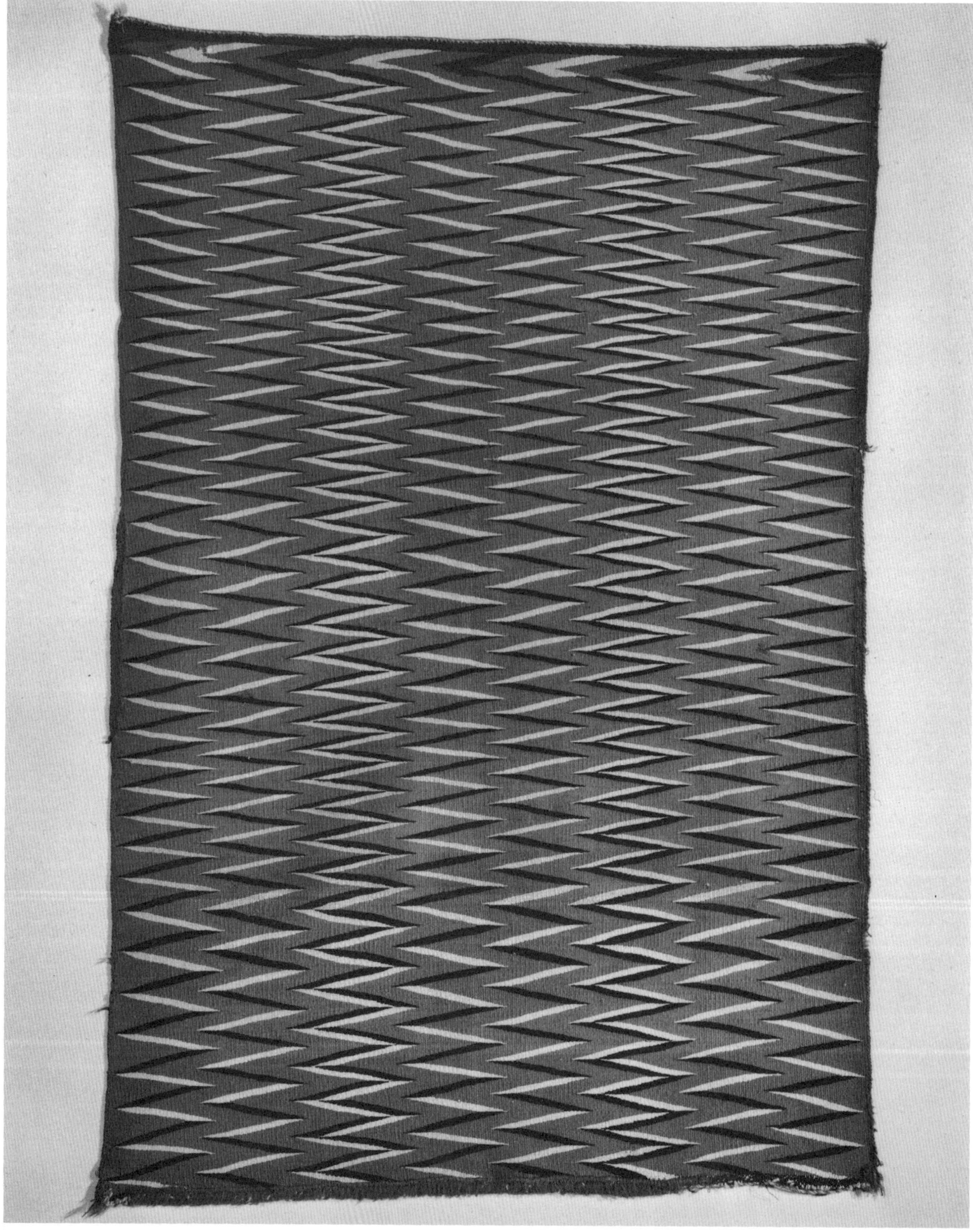

48. Serape Child's Blanket 1865–1875

Although smaller in size, children's blankets parallel the style of larger blankets. They consistently exhibit a high quality of craftsmanship and a great delicacy of design. The Maxwell Collection, Maxwell Museum of Anthropology University of New Mexico, Albuquerque

Length 57 in. (145.0 cm.)
Width 33 in. (83.5 cm.)

		WOOL	DYE
WARP	14/inch	Handspun	None
WEFT			
Blue	32/inch	Handspun	Indigo
Pink	32/inch	Recarded	Cochineal
Red	32/inch	Unraveled	Cochineal
White	32/inch	Handspun	None

49. Terraced Child's Blanket 1870–1880

Although small in size, this blanket displays the design complexity of larger blankets of the same period. Taylor Museum of the Colorado Springs Fine Arts Center

Length 50 in. (127.0 cm.)
Width 31 in. (78.5 cm.)

		WOOL	DYE
WARP	11/inch	Handspun	None
WEFT			
Blue	31/inch	Handspun	Indigo
Red	31/inch	Unraveled	?
White	31/inch	Handspun	None

50. Eye-Dazzler 1885–1890

When aniline dyed blankets were first produced, the early traders found the intensity of their colors garish. Time has radically altered the character of this aniline dyed blanket. Uneven fading has brought out the randomness of the dyeing and has softened the effect, giving it new complexity, range, and subtlety. Field Museum of Natural History, Chicago

Length 81 in. (206.0 cm.)
Width 54 in. (137.0 cm.)

		WOOL	DYE
WARP	8/inch	Handspun	None
WEFT			
Blue-Green	14/inch	Handspun	Aniline
Green	14/inch	Handspun	Aniline
Green-Yellow	14/inch	Handspun	Aniline
Grey	14/inch	Handspun	Aniline
Red	14/inch	Handspun	Aniline
Purple (light & dark)	14/inch	Handspun	Aniline

51. Eye-Dazzler 1880–1890

In this extremely energetic and visually engulfing eye-dazzler, a traditional design—the terrace pattern—all but disappears in a maze of new aniline colors. Anthony Berlant, Santa Monica, California

Length $87\frac{1}{2}$ in. (172.5 cm.)
Width 63 in. (160.0 cm.)

		WOOL	DYE
WARP	5/inch	Handspun	None
WEFT			
Brown	9/inch	Handspun	Aniline
Light Brown	9/inch	Handspun	Aniline
Grey	9/inch	Handspun	Aniline
Orange	9/inch	Handspun	Aniline
Red-Orange	9/inch	Handspun	Aniline
Yellow	9/inch	Handspun	Aniline
White	9/inch	Handspun	None

52. Chief Pattern Blanket—3rd Phase 1880–1890

In this third phase chief pattern blanket there is no longer a sense that the stripes are overlaid by the diamond shapes. Instead, an even balance has been achieved. Anthony Berlant, Santa Monica, California

Length $59^{1}/_{2}$ in. (151.0 cm.)
Width $76^{1}/_{2}$ in. (194.5 cm.)

		WOOL	DYE
WARP	9/inch	Handspun	None
WEFT			
Black	21/inch	Handspun	Native
Brown	21/inch	Handspun	None
Green	21/inch	Handspun	Aniline
Grey	21/inch	Handspun	None
Orange	21/inch	Handspun	Aniline
Red	21/inch	Handspun	Aniline

53. Eye-Dazzler 1885–1895

The sharp contrasts between black and white stripes and red and green diamonds create an almost dizzying vibration. An additional shimmer is produced by the very fine serration of diamond borders and by the slight misalignment of the stripes. The explosiveness of the entire design is held in check by dark red bands and the occasional interweaving of foreground and background elements. Anthony Berlant, Santa Monica, California

Length 74 in. (185.0 cm.)
Width 51 in. (130.0 cm.)

		WOOL	DYE
WARP	11/inch	Handspun	None
WEFT			
Black	25/inch	4-Ply	Aniline
Green	25/inch	4-Ply	Aniline
Red	25/inch	4-Ply	Aniline
White	25/inch	4-Ply	None

54. Banded 1870–1875

The Navajos, always able to adopt a foreign design, have in this example used the Pendleton blanket as a point of departure. The flat, static printed quality of the Pendleton is here infused with the Navajo sense of form and color. Millicent A. Rogers Memorial Museum, Inc., Taos, New Mexico

Length 70½ in. (178.0 cm.)
Width 50 in. (127.0 cm.)

		WOOL	DYE
WARP	11/inch	Handspun	None
WEFT			
Brown	21/inch	Handspun	None
Blue	21/inch	Handspun	Indigo
Green	21/inch	Handspun	?
Grey	21/inch	Handspun	None
Orange-Red	21/inch	Handspun	Aniline
Red	23/inch	Unraveled	Cochineal

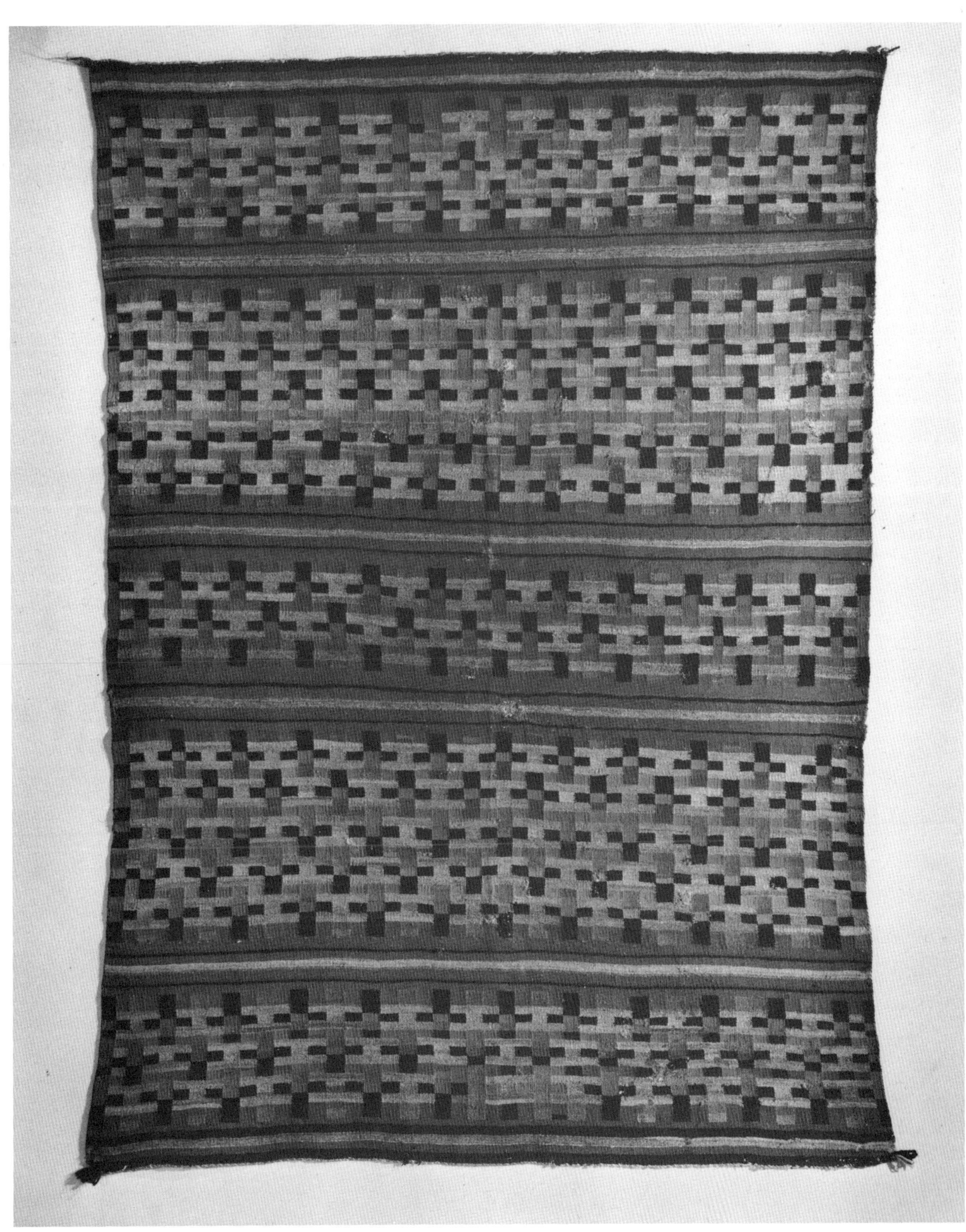

55. Banded 1875–1880

The banded style became common in the 1870s. In this example blue and green zig-zag motifs have been included in the stripe grid. Field Museum of Natural History, Chicago

Length 68 in. (173.0 cm.)
Width 54 in. (137.0 cm.)

		WOOL	DYE
WARP	7/inch	Handspun	None
WEFT			
Blue	16/inch	Handspun	Indigo
Red	16/inch	Handspun	Aniline
Yellow-Green	16/inch	Handspun	Aniline
White	16/inch	Handspun	None

56. Banded 1880–1890

Early designs were often carried into later periods. Such is the case in this example in which the colors, scale, and lack of edge detail indicate a date between 1880 and 1890. Kenneth Noland, New York

Length 59 in. (149.5 cm.)
Width $38^{1}/_{2}$ in. (97.0 cm.)

		WOOL	DYE
WARP	9/inch	Handspun	None
WEFT			
Black	16/inch	Handspun	Aniline
Pink	16/inch	Handspun	Aniline
Purple	16/inch	Handspun	Aniline
Red	16/inch	Handspun	Aniline
White	16/inch	Handspun	None
Yellow	16/inch	Handspun	Aniline

57. Terraced Child's Blanket 1875–1885

The terraced stripes of this blanket are viewed not as a succession of individual elements, but as parts of an overall rhythmical design. Southwest Museum, Los Angeles

Length 54 in. (137.0 cm.)
Width 34 in. (86.0 cm.)

		WOOL	DYE
WARP	9/inch	Handspun	None
WEFT			
Green-Blue	28/inch	Handspun	Aniline
Green	28/inch	Handspun	Aniline
Grey (faded purple)	28/inch	Handspun	Aniline
Red	28/inch	Handspun	Aniline
White	28/inch	Handspun	None
Yellow	28/inch	Handspun	Aniline

58. Child's Blanket 1880–1890

Sparseness of pattern elements makes particularly apparent the color reversals occurring in the chevrons. Such reversals are a common element in Navajo design schemes. Anthony Berlant, Santa Monica, California

Length 53 in. (134.5 cm.)
Width 36½ in. (93.0 cm.)

		COTTON	DYE
WARP	9/inch	4-Ply	None
WEFT		WOOL	
Purple	24/inch	4-Ply	Aniline
Red	24/inch	4-Ply	Aniline
White	24/inch	4-Ply	None

59. Hudson Bay Style 1880–1890

When we first discovered an example of this type, we felt it to be a completely unique blanket. Our subsequent studies revealed five others. The design is remarkably close to that of the Hudson Bay blanket, which suggests it provided the model. The blanket gains remarkable impact using sparse means. The large, expansive white field offers an excellent opportunity to study the lazy line weaving structure and handspun yarn. Georgia O'Keeffe, Abiquiu, New Mexico

Length $97^1/_2$ in. (248.0 cm.)
Width 63 in. (160.3 cm.)

		WOOL	DYE
WARP	4/inch	Handspun	None
WEFT			
Brown	7/inch	Handspun	None
White	7/inch	Handspun	None

60. Flag 1870–1885

The American flag had a special appeal to the Navajos as it has a striking similarity to the chief pattern blanket. A photograph dated 1873 of Governor W. F. A. Arny and a Navajo weaver shows a similar example.[22] Millicent A. Rogers Memorial Museum, Inc., Taos, New Mexico

Length 23 3/4 in. (60.5 cm.)
Width 56 1/2 in. (143.5 cm.)

		WOOL	DYE
WARP	10/inch	Handspun	None
WEFT			
Blue	20/inch	Handspun	Indigo
Red	20–30/inch	4-Ply	Aniline
White	20–28/inch	Handspun	None

61. Pictorial Style 1880–1890

In the 1880s the Navajos began to employ pictographic designs as major motifs in their blankets. In this example, the horse—a Navajo symbol of wealth—is treated in a stylized manner. The horses are rendered by lines built up with traditionally stepped edges. Taylor Museum of the Colorado Springs Fine Arts Center

Length 84 in. (213.5 cm.)
Width $51^{1}/_{2}$ in. (131.0 cm.)

		WOOL	DYE
WARP	5/inch	Handspun	None
WEFT			
Black	11/inch	Handspun	Aniline
Blue	11/inch	Handspun	Indigo
Red	11/inch	Handspun	Aniline
White	11/inch	Handspun	None
Yellow	11/inch	Handspun	Aniline

62. Eye-Dazzler 1885–1890

As in all eye-dazzlers, the colors in this example are brilliant and explosive, the execution loose and rapid, and the design seems capable of infinite extension. Color is pre-eminent. Anthony Berlant, Santa Monica, California

Length 78 in. (198.0 cm.)
Width 67 in. (120.5 cm.)

		WOOL	DYE
WARP	4/inch	Handspun	None
WEFT			
Black	10/inch	Handspun	Aniline
Orange	10/inch	Handspun	Aniline
Red-Orange	10/inch	Handspun	Aniline
Yellow	10/inch	Handspun	Aniline
White	10/inch	Handspun	None

63. Eye-Dazzler 1880–1890

An unexpected shift in a motif, used to add a slight variation, is common as a detail in Navajo blankets. Used here as the central motif, it is amplified to produce a startling effect. Anthony Berlant, Santa Monica, California

Length 87 in. (221.0 cm.)
Width 59 in. (149.5 cm.)

		WOOL	DYE
WARP	6/inch	Handspun	None
WEFT			
Black	8/inch	Handspun	Aniline
Brown	8/inch	Handspun	None
Red	8/inch	Handspun	Aniline
White	8/inch	Handspun	None
Yellow	8/inch	Handspun	Aniline

64. Late Serape Style 1875–1885

The unusual repetition of the simple chevron motif, the limited color combination, and the serrated edge produce a design of great strength. The color striations in the background present a subtle contrast.
Anthony Berlant, Santa Monica, California

Length 81 in. (206.0 cm.)
Width 56 in. (142.5 cm.)

		WOOL	DYE
WARP	8/inch	4-Ply	None
WEFT			
Black	24/inch	4-Ply	Aniline
Blue	24/inch	4-Ply	Aniline
Red	24/inch	3-Ply	Aniline
Red	24/inch	4-Ply	Aniline
White	24/inch	4-Ply	None

65. Wedge-Weave Style 1885–1895

The unusually large scale of the design elements and the variations of tone within the blue and red add to the animated effect of the blanket. Wharton James, who wrote the first major book about Indian blankets, referred to wedge-weaves as lightning blankets.[23] Anthony Berlant, Santa Monica, California

Length 78 in. (198.0 cm.)
Width 59 in. (149.5 cm.)

		WOOL	DYE
WARP	6/inch	Handspun	None
WEFT			
Black	9/inch	Handspun	None
Blue	9/inch	Handspun	Aniline
Red	9/inch	Handspun	Aniline
White	9/inch	Handspun	None

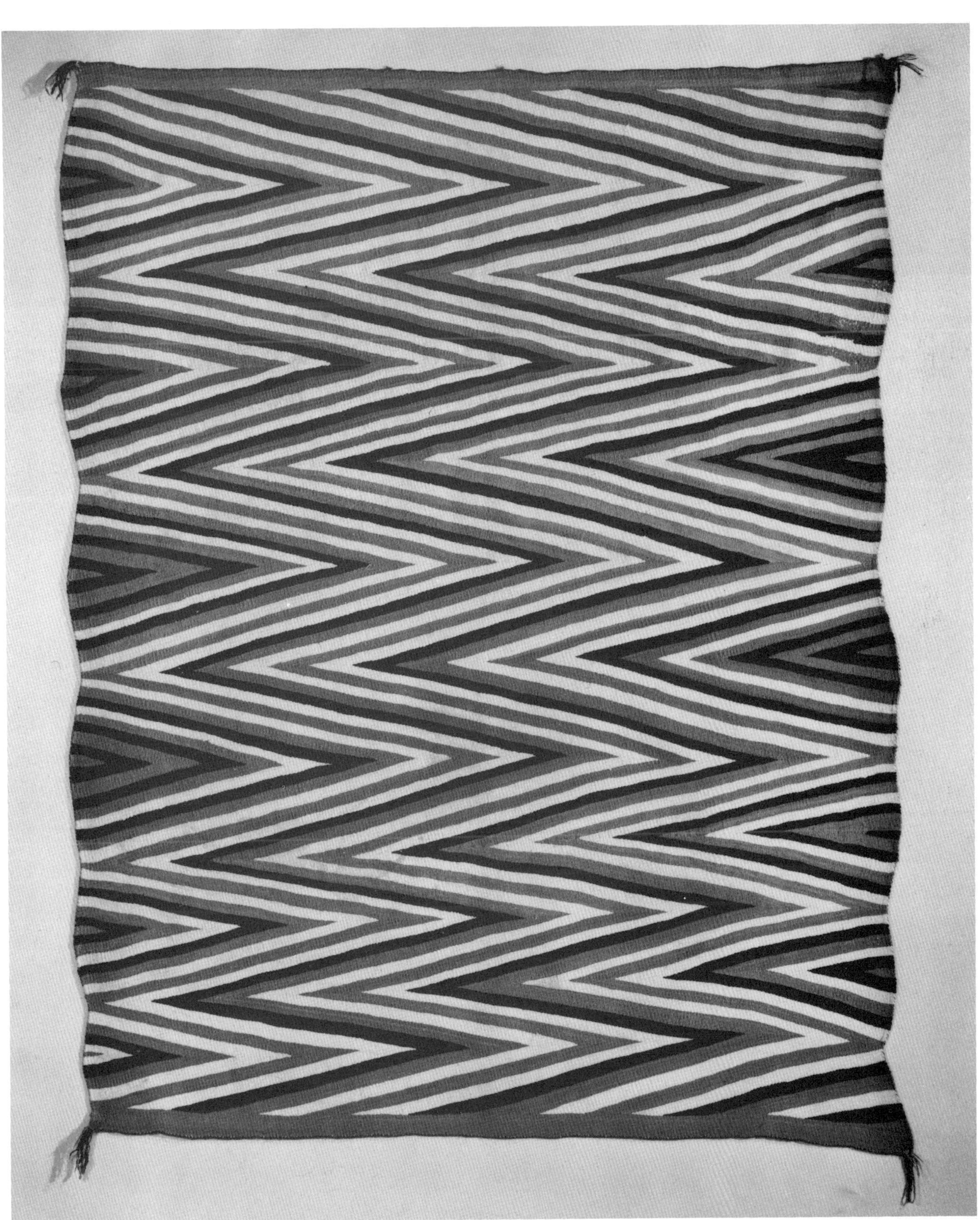

66. Wedge-Weave Style 1880–1890

A combination of wedge-weave and plain stripe, as in this example, was more common than allover wedge-weave. The color in this instance has faded a great deal, producing an extraordinary degree of delicacy.
Anthony Berlant, Santa Monica, California

Length 80½ in. (204.5 cm.)
Width 53 in. (134.5 cm.)

		WOOL	DYE
WARP	7/inch	Handspun	None
WEFT			
Black	13/inch	Handspun	Aniline
Grey	13/inch	Handspun	Aniline
Orange	13/inch	Handspun	Aniline
Pink	13/inch	Handspun	Aniline
White	13/inch	Handspun	None
Yellow	13/inch	Handspun	Aniline

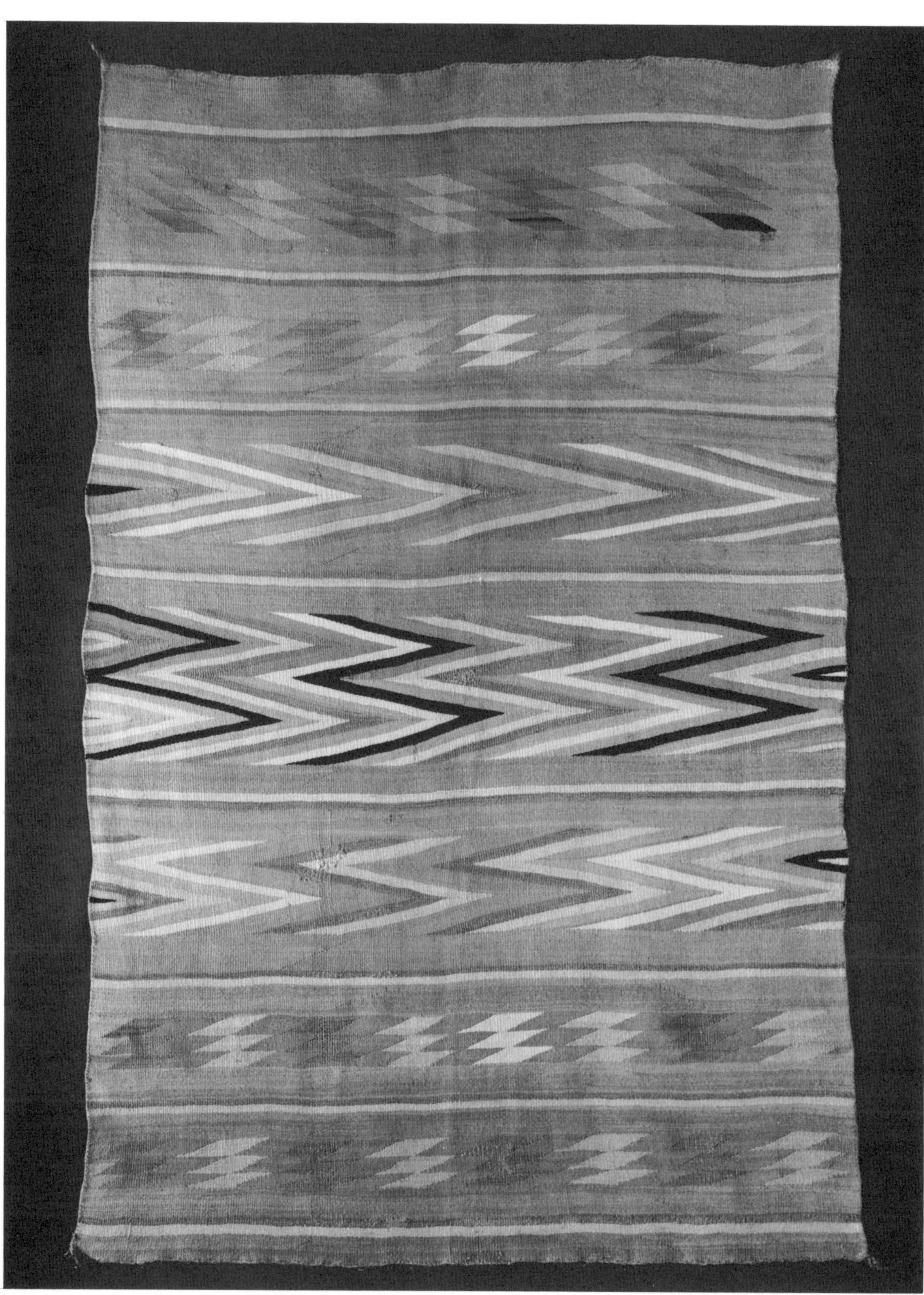

67. Wedge-Weave Style 1885–1895

The diagonal orientation of this blanket heightens the sense of agitation inherent in the wedge-weave style. Anthony Berlant, Santa Monica, California

Length 67 in. (170.5 cm.)
Width 62 in. (157.0 cm.)

		WOOL	DYE
WARP	6/inch	Handspun	None
WEFT			
Light Brown	12/inch	Handspun	None
Blue	12/inch	Handspun	Aniline
Orange	12/inch	Handspun	Aniline
White	12/inch	Handspun	None
Yellow	12/inch	Handspun	Aniline

68. Banded 1880–1890

The large banded stripe tradition, found in early blankets, continued to be used late into the nineteenth century as in this example of a loosely-woven oversize blanket. Frank Stella, New York

Length 96½ in. (245.0 cm.)
Width 55 in. (139.5 cm.)

		WOOL	DYE
WARP	4/inch	Handspun	None
WEFT			
Red	9/inch	Handspun	Aniline
White	9/inch	Handspun	None

69. Eye-Dazzler 1880–1890

The combination of acid and mellow color is found most frequently in the 1880s. Anthony Berlant, Santa Monica, California

Length $84^{1}/_{4}$ in. (214.0 cm.)
Width $59^{1}/_{4}$ in. (150.5 cm.)

		WOOL	DYE
WARP	6/inch	Handspun	None
WEFT			
Black	9/inch	Handspun	Aniline
Brown	9/inch	Handspun	Aniline
Dark Brown	9/inch	Handspun	Aniline
Grey	9/inch	Handspun	Aniline
Orange	9/inch	Handspun	Aniline
Purple	9/inch	Handspun	Aniline
Red	9/inch	Handspun	Aniline
Yellow-Green	9/inch	Handspun	Aniline
White	9/inch	Handspun	None

70. Chief Pattern Blanket—3rd Phase 1890–1895

In this late chief pattern blanket, the diamonds of the earlier third phase have been replaced by crosses. In addition, the black and white stripes have ceased to function as a background grid and have begun to work as overlay elements. Millicent A. Rogers Memorial Museum, Inc., Taos, New Mexico

Length 54½ in. (138.7 cm.)
Width 63 in. (160.0 cm.)

		WOOL	DYE
WARP	10/inch	4-Ply	None
WEFT			
Black	26/inch	4-Ply	Aniline
Blue-Green	26/inch	4-Ply	Aniline
Green	26/inch	4-Ply	Aniline
Purple	26/inch	4-Ply	Aniline
Red	22/inch	4-Ply	Aniline
White	28/inch	4-Ply	None

71. Banded 1880–1895

The lozenge motif used in the banded style commonly occurs in the late 1880s and early 1890s. The alternating bands give a diagonal movement to this example. The Heard Museum, Phoenix

Length 81 in. (205.5 cm.)
Width $56^{1}/_{2}$ in. (143.0 cm.)

		WOOL	DYE
WARP	8/inch	Handspun	None
WEFT			
Black	17/inch	Handspun	Aniline
Blue	17/inch	Handspun	Aniline
Brown	17/inch	Handspun	Aniline
Red	17/inch	Handspun	Aniline
Orange-Yellow	17/inch	Handspun	Aniline
Yellow	17/inch	Handspun	Aniline
White	17/inch	Handspun	None

72. Wedge-Weave Style 1885–1895

The large diagonals of this blanket are created by a wedge-weave technique in which the warp is pulled from side to side. As a result of this dislocation, the edges are scalloped. Anthony Berlant, Santa Monica, California

Length 76½ in. (194.5 cm.)
Width 61½ in. (157.0 cm.)

		WOOL	DYE
WARP	9/inch	Handspun	None
WEFT			
Blue	16/inch	Handspun	Aniline
Red	16/inch	Handspun	Aniline
White	16/inch	Handspun	None

73. Transitional Style 1885–1895

The erratic distribution of color, the absence of a center, and the ambiguity of foreground and background in this example produce a complex field without the center-oriented organization of earlier blankets. Anthony Berlant, Santa Monica, California

Length 82 in. (208.0 cm.)
Width 52 in. (132.0 cm.)

		WOOL	DYE
WARP	7/inch	Handspun	None
WEFT			
Black	8/inch	Handspun	Aniline
Browns	8/inch	Handspun	None
Red	8/inch	Handspun	Aniline
White	8/inch	Handspun	None
Yellow	8/inch	Handspun	Aniline

74. Eye-Dazzler 1890–1895

A change from a horizontal to a vertical format occurred in the blankets of the 1890s. Donald Judd, New York

Length 73½ in. (187.0 cm.)
Width 55 in. (139.7 cm.)

		WOOL	DYE
WARP	6/inch	Handspun	None
WEFT			
Blue	13/inch	Handspun	Aniline
Blue-Green	13/inch	Handspun	Aniline
Green-Blue	13/inch	Handspun	Aniline
Orange	13/inch	Handspun	Aniline
Pink	13/inch	Handspun	Aniline
Reds	13/inch	Handspun	Aniline
Yellow	13/inch	Handspun	Aniline

75. Transitional Style 1885–1895

Although this blanket was made between 1885 and 1895, it is calmer and more controlled in aspect than most blankets of this period.
Jasper Johns, New York

Length 92 in. (233.5 cm.)
Width 62¼ in. (158.0 cm.)

		WOOL	DYE
WARP	9/inch	Handspun	None
WEFT			
Black	18/inch	Handspun	Aniline
Brown	18/inch	Handspun	None
Green	18/inch	Handspun	Aniline
Yellow-Green	18/inch	Handspun	Aniline
Grey	18/inch	Handspun	Aniline
Red (various shades)	18/inch	Handspun	Aniline
Orange-Red	18/inch	Handspun	Aniline
Yellow-Orange	18/inch	Handspun	Aniline
White	18/inch	Handspun	None

76. Eye-Dazzler 1885–1895

The uniqueness of this eye-dazzler results from its strange combination of colors. The mechanical repetitiousness of pattern, flatness of color, and outlining of forms are all typical of Germantown blankets. The four-ply Germantown yarn, seen in the detail (opposite), has an evenness of texture and color density. Anthony Berlant, Santa Monica, California

Length 71½ in. (181.5 cm.)
Width 48½ in. (123.0 cm.)

		COTTON	DYE
WARP	11/inch	3-Ply	None
WEFT		WOOL	
Black	20/inch	4-Ply	Aniline
Green (dark)	20/inch	4-Ply	Aniline
Green (light)	20/inch	4-Ply	Aniline
Orange-Red	20/inch	4-Ply	Aniline
Orange-Yellow	20/inch	4-Ply	Aniline
Red	20/inch	4-Ply	Aniline
White	20/inch	4-Ply	None

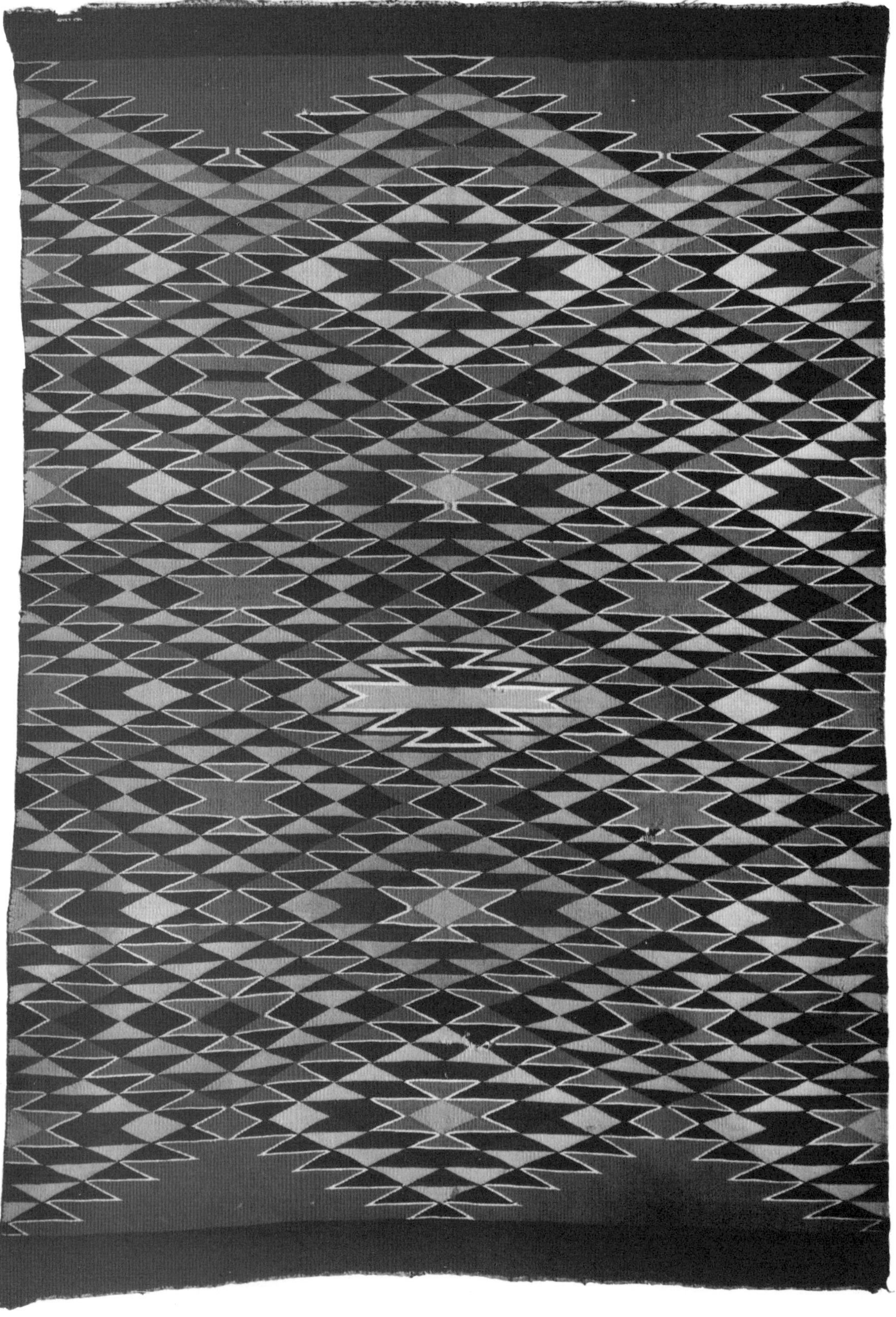

NO. 916-15
1
MADE IN U.S.A.
2
3
4
5
6
7

77. Eye-Dazzler 1890–1895

The design of this blanket is built from two elements, the diamond and the enlarged serrated edge. Variegated yarn, frequently employed in Mexican serapes, is used with restraint in this otherwise unrestrained eye-dazzler. Anthony Berlant, Santa Monica, California

Length 70 in. (178.0 cm.)
Width $55^{1}/_{4}$ in. (140.0 cm.)

		WOOL	DYE
WARP	11/inch	4-Ply	None
WEFT			
Black	23/inch	4-Ply	Aniline
Blue-Green	23/inch	4-Ply	Aniline
Yellow-Green	23/inch	4-Ply	Aniline
Purple	23/inch	4-Ply	Aniline
Red	23/inch	4-Ply	Aniline
Dark Red	23/inch	4-Ply	Aniline
Variegated	23/inch	4-Ply	Aniline
White	23/inch	4-Ply	None
Yellow	23/inch	4-Ply	Aniline

78. Transitional Style 1895–1900

This example was woven during the period of transition when the weaving of blankets began to be replaced by the making of rugs. The eccentricity of the design is characteristic of the 1890s. Anthony Berlant, Santa Monica, California

Length 85½ in. (218.0 cm.)
Width 51 in. (129.5 cm.)

		WOOL	DYE
WARP	6/inch	Handspun	None
WEFT			
Dark Brown	8/inch	Handspun	None
Light Brown	8/inch	Handspun	None
Red	8/inch	Handspun	Aniline
White	8/inch	Handspun	None

79. Eye-Dazzler 1890–1900

This blanket type, commissioned by Lorenzo Hubbel and C. N. Cotton at their Ganado Trading Post in the 1890s, was an adaptation of an earlier style of the 1870s (see plate 38). The use of letters was an eccentric design variant introduced during the trading post era.
Anthony Berlant, Santa Monica, California

Length 74½ in. (189.5 cm.)
Width 52 in. (132.0 cm.)

		WOOL	DYE
WARP	8/inch	Handspun	None
WEFT			
Black	29/inch	4-Ply	Aniline
Purple	29/inch	4-Ply	Aniline
Red	29/inch	4-Ply	Aniline
White	29/inch	4-Ply	None

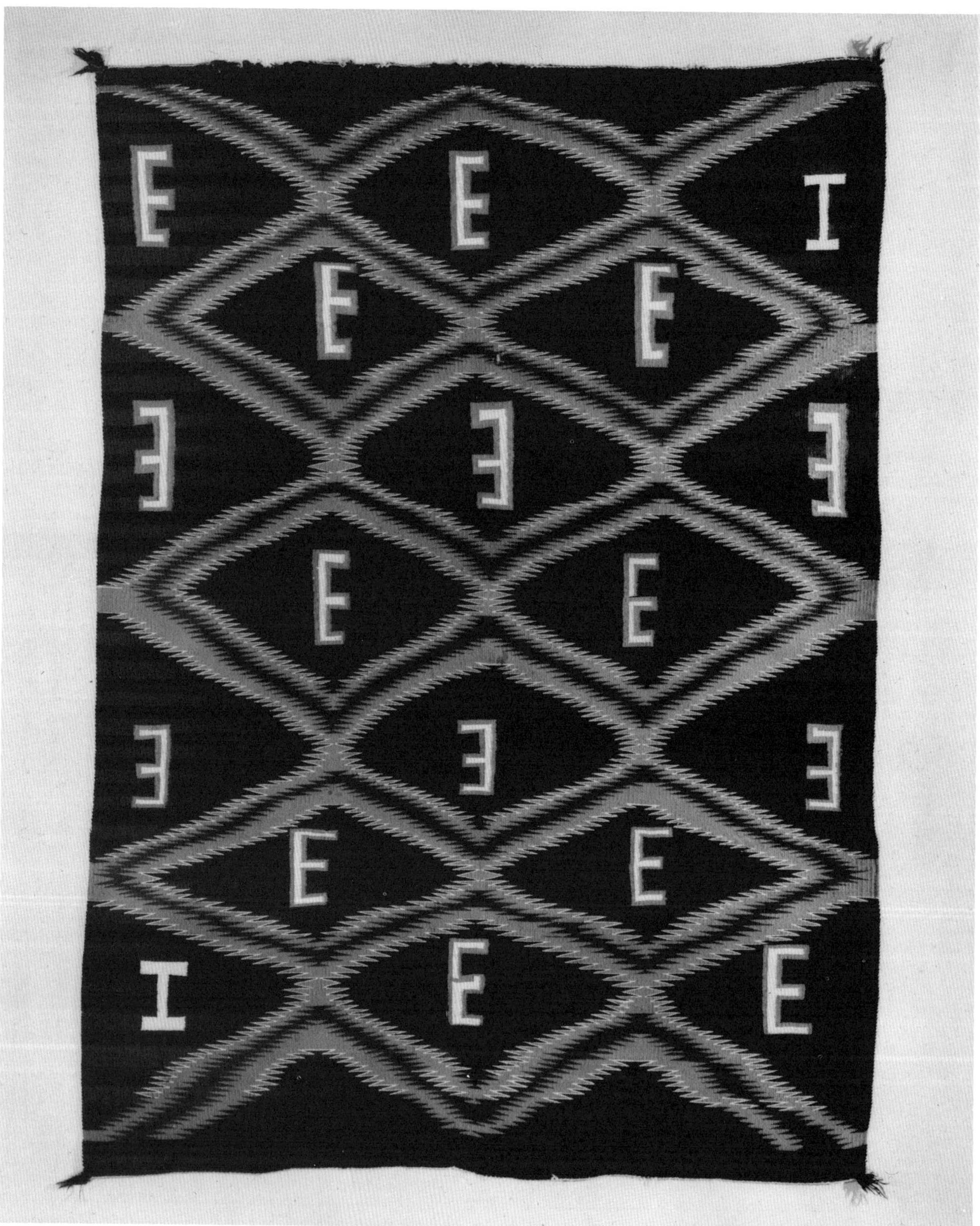

80. Transitional Style 1890–1900

Although the nine-point motif of the chief pattern blanket still remains, the stripes have all but disappeared from this transitional period example. Variations of natural grey have replaced color so that the lazy line structure creates a richly differentiated field. Anthony Berlant, Santa Monica, California

Length 81 in. (206.0 cm.)
Width 81 in. (206.0 cm.)

		WOOL	DYE
WARP	8/inch	Handspun	White
WEFT			
Black	19/inch	Handspun	?
Grey	19/inch	Handspun	None
Red	19/inch	Handspun	Aniline
White	19/inch	Handspun	None

81. Rug 1885–1895

The size of this example clearly indicates it was woven to be used as a floor covering. Instead of enlarging the elements to fill this enormous Germantown piece, the weaver divided it into nine sections. Each section has a distinct design quality which makes the piece, in a sense, a catalog of the various dominant designs of the period. An almost identical example of this type is found in the Maxwell Museum of Anthropology. The size and eccentricity of these remarkable pieces would suggest that they were woven by the same weaver. Anthony Berlant, Santa Monica, California

Length 135 in. (343.0 cm.)
Width 133 in. (338.0 cm.)

		COTTON	DYE
WARP	11/inch	3-Ply	None
WEFT		WOOL	
Black	25/inch	4-Ply	Aniline
Blue	25/inch	4-Ply	Aniline
Green	25/inch	4-Ply	Aniline
Orange	25/inch	4-Ply	Aniline
Purple	25/inch	4-Ply	Aniline
Red	25/inch	4-Ply	Aniline
White	25/inch	4-Ply	None
Yellow	25/inch	4-Ply	Aniline

Notes

Frontispiece: Gladys A. Reichard, *Spider-woman,* (frontispiece). New York: The Macmillian Company, 1934.

1. Charles Avery Amsden, *Navaho Weaving, Its Technic and Its History* (Glorieta, New Mexico: The Rio Grande Press, 1934), p. 160; Ruth Underhill, *The Navajos* (Norman, Oklahoma: University of Oklahoma Press, 1956), p. 127.

2. Rachel Sherman Thorndike, ed., *The Sherman Letters: Correspondence between General and Senator Sherman from 1837 to 1891* (New York, 1894), pp. 318–19; Amsden, *op. cit.,* p. 35.

3. Underhill, *op. cit.,* p. 35.

4. Herbert E. Bolton, ed., *Spanish Explorations in the Southwest, 1542–1706* (New York: Charles Scribner's Sons, 1916), p. 202; George P. Hammond and Agopito Rey, "Gallegos' Relation of the Rodriguez Expedition to New Mexico" (Historical Society of New Mexico, 1927), p. 19; Underhill, *op. cit.,* p. 34.

5. Lansing B. Bloom, "Early Weaving in New Mexico," *The New Mexico Historical Review* 2 (July, 1927): 233.

6. Pedro Pino, *Exposición del Nuevo México* (Cadiz, Spain, 1812), p. 441; Amsden, *op. cit.,* p. 133.

7. See illustration, Amsden, *op. cit.,* plate 60; plate 63 illustrates another example of a shoulder blanket from the collection of the Museum of New Mexico.

8. *Ibid.,* plate 62.

9. *Ibid.,* pp. 183–84.

10. *Ibid.,* plate 78. Amsden suggests that aniline dyes may have been obtained at Bosque Redondo.

11. *Songs of the Tewa,* translated by Herbert Joseph Spinden (New York: The Brooklyn Museum, 1933).

12. Amsden, *op. cit.,* p. 97.

13. In her book on Rio Grande textiles, soon to be published, E. Boyd Hall suggests that sometime around 1830 elaborate diamond-motif blankets were brought north from Mexico and began to be copied by the Spanish weavers in New Mexico.

14. Other fragments from the collection are illustrated in Amsden, *op. cit.,* plates 61 and 62.

15. Aileen A. O'Bryon, *The Dîné Origin Myths of the Navajo Indians* (Washington, D.C.: Smithsonian Institution, 1956), p. 56.

16. Franciscan Fathers, *An Ethnologic Dictionary of the Navajo Language* (St. Michaels, Arizona: St. Michaels Press, 1910), p. 222.

17. See illustration, Amsden, *op. cit.,* plate 75, of blankets collected by Thomas S. Twiss in the 1860's at Fort Laramie, Wyoming. Museum of the American Indian, Heye Foundation Cat. 10–8457.

18. *Ibid.,* p. 182.

19. We are grateful to Mr. David Brugge, Curator of the Ganado Trading Post, for this information.

20. See, for example, illustration on p. 12 of this catalog, and Amsden, *op. cit.,* plate 82.

21. Amsden, *op. cit.,* plate 102.

22. Amsden, *op. cit.,* plate 114.

23. George Wharton James, *Indian Blankets and Their Makers* (Chicago: Tudor Publishing, 1937).

Ah-del-staline, or Straight Shooter, taken at Keams Canyon about 1900; courtesy of History Division, Natural History Museum of Los Angeles County. Photograph by A. C. Vroman

Bibliography

AMSDEN, CHARLES AVERY. *Navaho Weaving, Its Technic and Its History.* Glorieta, New Mexico: The Rio Grande Press, 1934.

BLOOM, LANSING B. "Early Weaving in New Mexico." *The New Mexico Historical Review* 2 (July, 1927).

BLUNN, CECIL T. "Navaho Sheep." *The Journal of Heredity* 31 (March, 1940): 99–112.

BOLTON, HERBERT E., ed. *Spanish Explorations in the Southwest, 1542–1706.* New York: Charles Scribner's Sons, 1925.

BORN, WOLFGANG. "Scarlet." *Ciba Review,* no. 7 (March, 1938).

BRUGGE, DAVID; CARREL, T. LEE; and WATSON, EDITH. *Navajo Bibliography.* Window Rock, Arizona: Navajo Tribal Museum, 1967.

CALHOUN, JAMES J. *The Official Correspondence of James S. Calhoun While Indian Agent at Santa Fe and Superintendent of Indian Affairs in New Mexico.* Edited by Annie Heloise Abel. Washington, D.C., 1915.

CHEETHAM, FRANCIS T. "Kit Carson." *The New Mexico Historical Review* 1 (1926): 375–99.

CURTIS, EDWARD S. *The North American Indian* 20 vols. Cambridge: Harvard University Press, 1907–30.

DOUGLAS, FREDERICH. *The Navaho Indians.* Denver Art Museum Leaflet, no. 21, April, 1931.

———. *Many Types of Pueblo Cotton Textiles.* Denver Art Museum Leaflet, January, 1940.

DUTTON, BERTHA. *Navaho Weaving Today.* Santa Fe, New Mexico: Museum of New Mexico Press, 1961.

FORMER, MALCOLM. "Navaho Archeology of Upper Blanco and Largo Canyons." *American Antiquity* 8 (July, 1942): 65–79.

FRANCISCAN FATHERS. *An Ethnologic Dictionary of the Navaho Language.* St. Michaels, Arizona: St. Michaels Press, 1910.

GILPIN, LAURA. *The Enduring Navaho.* Austin, Texas: University of Texas Press, 1968.

GODDARD, PLINY EARLE. "Navaho Blankets." *American Museum Journal* 10: 201–11.

———. "Navaho Texts." *Anthropological Papers of American Museum of Natural History.* New York: American Museum of Natural History, 1933.

GREGG, JOSIAH. *The Commerce of the Prairies.* New York: Citadel Press, 1968.

HAMMOND, GEORGE P., and REY, AGOPITO. "Gallegos' Relation of the Rodriguez Expedition to New Mexico." Historical Society of New Mexico, 1927.

HILL, WILLARD. "Navaho Trading and Trading Ritual: A Study of Cultural Dynamics." *Southwestern Journal of Anthropology* 4 (1948): 371–94.

———. "Some Navaho Culture Changes During Two Centuries." *Smithsonian Miscellaneous Collection,* no. 98 (1940), pp. 371–96.

HUBBELL, JOHN LORENZO. "Fifty Years an Indian Trader (As Told to John Edwin Hagg)." *Touring Topics* 22 (December, 1930): 24–29, 51.

JAMES, GEORGE WHARTON. *Indian Blankets and Their Makers.* Chicago: Tudor Publishing, 1937.

JEANCON, JEAN, and DOUGLAS, FREDERICH. *Navaho Spinning, Dyeing, and Weaving.* Denver Art Museum Leaflet, no. 3, April, 1930.

JONES, COURTNEY. "Spindle Spinning: Navaho Style." *Plateau* 18 (January, 1946): 43–51.

KENT, KATE PECK. "The Cultivation and Weaving of Cotton in the Pre-Historic United States." *Transactions of the American Philosophical Society* n.s. vol. 47, pt. 3 (1957): 457–733.

KLUCKHORN, CLYDE, and LEIGHTON, DOROTHEA. *The Navaho.* Garden City, New York: Doubleday & Co., Inc., 1962.

KLUCKHORN, CLYDE, and SPENCER, KATHERINE. *A Bibliography of the Navaho Indians.* New York: J. J. Augustin, 1940.

LETTERMAN, JONATHAN. "Sketches of the Navaho Tribe of Indians, Territory of New Mexico." *Tenth Annual Report of the Smithsonian Institution* (1855), pp. 283–97.

LUOMALA, KATHERINE. *Navaho Life of Yesterday and Today.* Berkeley, California: U.S. Department of the Interior, Park Service, 1938.

MATTHEWS, WASHINGTON. "Navaho Weavers." *Third Annual Report of the Bureau of Ethnology to the Secretary of the Smithsonian Institute* (1884), pp. 371–91.

———. *Navaho Legends.* Boston: American Folklore Society, 1897.

MATTHEWS, WASHINGTON, and GODDARD, PLINY EARLE., eds. "Navaho Myths, Prayers and Songs with Text and Translations." *University of California Publications in American Archeology and Ethnology* 5 (1907–10): 21–63.

MAXWELL, GILBERT S. *Navaho Rugs.* Palm Desert, California: Best-West Publications, 1963.

MERA, H. P. *The Alfred I. Barton Collection of Southwestern Textiles.* Santa Fe, New Mexico: San Vicente Foundation Inc., 1949.

———. *Navaho Textile Arts.* Santa Fe, New Mexico: Laboratory of Anthropology, 1947.

O'BRYON, AILEEN. *The Dîné Origin Myths of the Navaho Indians.* Washington, D.C.: Smithsonian Institution, 1956.

PINO, PEDRO B. *Exposición del Nuevo México.* Cadiz, Spain, 1812.

REICHARD, GLADYS A. *Spider Woman: A Story of Navaho Weavers and Charters.* New York: The Macmillan Company, 1934.

———. *Navaho Shepherd and Weaver.* New York: J. J. Augustin, 1936.

TERRELL, JOHN UPTON. *The Navajos: Past and Present of a Great People.* New York: Weybright and Talley, 1970.

THORNDIKE, RACHEL SHERMAN, ed. *The Sherman Letters: Correspondence between General and Senator Sherman from 1837 to 1891.* New York; 1894.

UNDERHILL, RUTH M. *The Navajos.* Norman, Oklahoma: University of Oklahoma Press, 1956.

———. *Red Man's America.* Chicago: University of Chicago Press, 1953.

UTLEY, ROBERT M. "The Reservation Trader in Navaho History." (National Park Service) *El Palacio* 68 (Spring, 1961): 5–27.

VETTERLI, W. A. "The History of Indigo." *Ciba Review* 85 (April, 1951): 3066–71.

VOGT, EVAN Z., and ROBERTS, JOHN M. "A Study of Values." *Scientific America,* July, 1956, pp. 25–31.

VOGT, EVANS, and KLUCKHOHN, CLYDE. *Navaho Means People.* Cambridge, Massachusetts: Harvard University Press, 1951.

WATKINS, FRANCES E. *The Navaho.* Southwest Museum Leaflet, no. 16. Los Angeles, California, 1942.

WISSLER, CLARK, *The American Indian.* New York: Douglas C. McMurtrie, 1917.

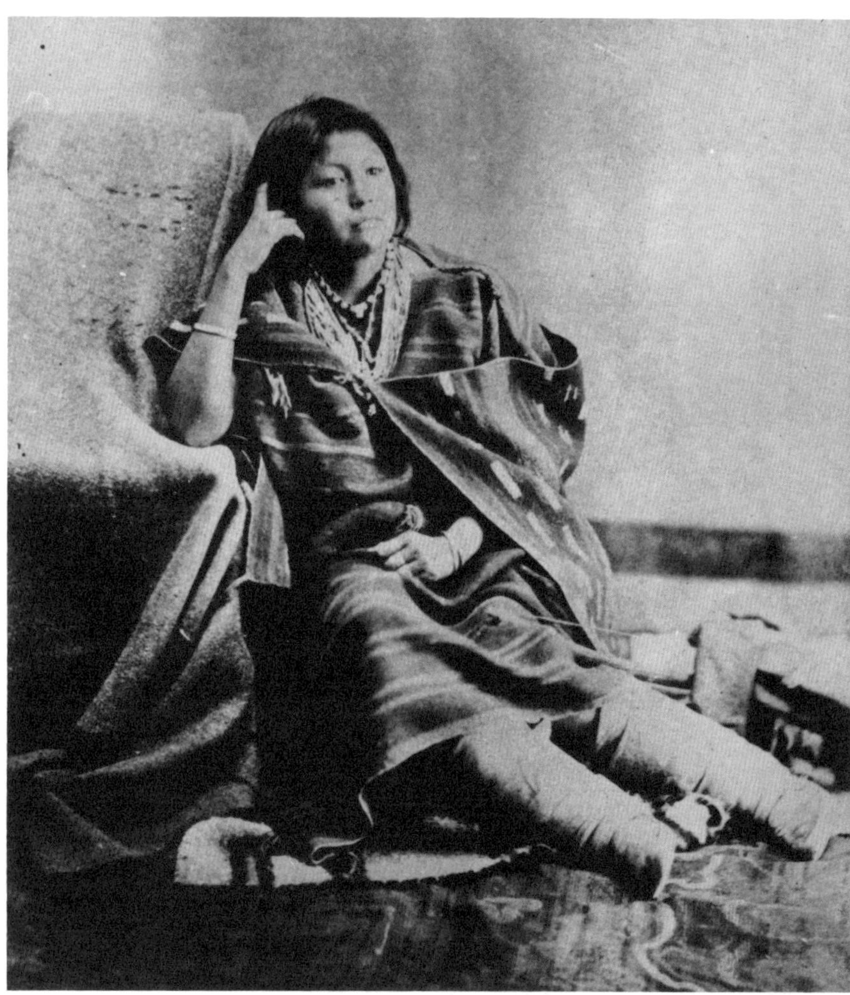

Navajo girl from about the time of Bosque Redondo; courtesy of Museum of New Mexico

Designed in Los Angeles by Louis Danziger. All text set in Linotron 505 Palatino by Black Dot, Crystal Lake, Illinois. The catalog is printed on Navajo Text by Halliday Lithograph Corporation, Massachusetts. The color plates on Cameo Brilliant Dull by Princeton Polychrome, New Jersey. Photographs of blankets by John Gebhart, Los Angeles.